# This Is My Faith

*A personal guide to Confirmation*

*with an Order of Holy Communion*

## Douglas Dales

CANTERBURY
PRESS
Norwich

The Psalm quotations in Part Two
are taken from the Alternative Service Book 1980.
Bible quotations are taken from
the Revised English Bible.

The Communion Service (Order One) from Common
Worship: Services and Prayers for the Church of England
is © The Archbishops' Council 2000 and is reproduced
by permission.

Text © Douglas Dales 2000 and 2001
Illustrations © Paul Jenkins 2000

First published in 2003 by the Canterbury Press Norwich
(a publishing imprint of Hymns Ancient & Modern Ltd
a registered charity)
St. Mary's Works, St. Mary's Plain
Norwich, Norfolk, NR3 3BH

This enlarged edition first published in 2001.
Third impression 2004

A catalogue record for this book is available
from the British Library

ISBN 1–85311–536–3

Typeset by Regent Typesetting, London
Printed in Great Britain by
Biddles Ltd, King's Lynn, Norfolk

# Contents

**Part Four: Being with God**

# Author's Preface

This book is intended for young people who are preparing for Confirmation or simply thinking about being confirmed. It is also designed to be a spiritual handbook for them to use in the years after their Confirmation. Those who are preparing young people and adults for Confirmation in parishes and schools could also use the material as a resource.

It arises out of preparing teenagers for Confirmation over many years in two parishes and at Marlborough College. It owes a great deal to them for their kindness, interest and questions. I am grateful too for the advice and encouragement of my colleagues and friends, the Revd James Dickie and the Revd Henry Pearson.

The biblical references are from the Revised English Bible, and the prayers are drawn and adapted from Anglican and other sources.

The Bishop of Salisbury has very kindly contributed a brief introduction to Order One of the

Eucharist in *Common Worship*. I have chosen prayer B because it is closely modelled on the oldest known consecrating prayer, called the Hippolytan rite, which comes from Rome around 200 AD. It therefore underlies all the consecrating prayers of the Church, and affirms the deep unity in Christ which we experience when celebrating the Eucharist. It is printed at the end of this book as the goal of all our prayer and preparation.

Douglas Dales
*Marlborough, Easter 2001*

# Welcome to Confirmation

Confirmation is an opportunity for you to affirm your own Christian faith in a personal and informed way. It has existed in the Church for many centuries as the confirmation of what began with Baptism, which for many people still occurs when they are children. At Baptism, promises were made on your behalf that you would be brought up in the Christian faith. Confirmation is therefore the opportunity for you to renew these promises for yourself. A bishop, normally in the context of Holy Communion, administers confirmation in the Anglican Church.

No one is ever fully prepared for Confirmation in the sense that they feel that they understand everything about being a Christian. But Confirmation preparation should enable you to understand the essential elements of your faith and its meaning in your life, and should lay the basis for further growth in spiritual life and prayer. When you pass a driving test, you throw away the 'L' plates, but when you are confirmed you agree to wear them for life as a disciple of Christ!

---

**Pause for reflection**

*Why do I want to be confirmed?*

*Who or what has influenced me in my Christian faith?*

*Is being confirmed my own personal and free decision?*

---

In this little book we will explore what Christians believe, with special reference to the promises made at Baptism and Confirmation, and to the service of Holy Communion (sometimes called the Eucharist). The book should enable you to explain to your friends and family why you are a Christian. It will also help you to make decisions in a Christian spirit and to find a personal way of praying.

At its heart, Christianity is personal – a relationship with God in Jesus Christ, in which you come to feel loved and known by him. This relationship needs time and patience to grow and become secure. It must also be voluntary and loving, and there must be effective communication both ways.

Prayer is therefore time that a Christian sets aside for talking and listening to God. That is why time spent in prayer is never wasted, because it is time given to communicating with him. Many of the best relationships are lifelong ones, such as marriage, parent-child relationships and good friendships. A Christian's relationship with God is also a lifelong one, and Confirmation is an important milestone in its development.

### Prayer

Here is a prayer which you might like to memorize and say at the start of each day:

*O God, you have prepared for those who love you*
*such good things as pass our understanding;*
*pour into our hearts such love towards you,*
*that, loving you in all things and above all things,*
*we may obtain your promises,*
*which exceed all that we can desire;*
*through Jesus Christ our Lord.*
*Amen.*

*(Book of Common Prayer)*

# PART ONE

# Becoming a Christian

# What Is a Christian?

People were first called 'Christians' because they were seen to be followers of Jesus, whom they believed to be the Messiah. 'Messiah' is a Hebrew word that means 'God's chosen one'. The Greek translation of 'Messiah' is the word 'Christ'. You can read about these earliest Christians in the Acts of the Apostles in the New Testament.

One of the best summaries of how the earliest Christians believed in Jesus is found in the First Letter of St John (1 John 4:7–21). It makes a number of important statements that speak to us today.

It says, 'If anyone acknowledges that Jesus is God's Son, God dwells in him, and he in God.' This means that as Christians we believe that Jesus came from God and is his beloved Son – he came to make God known to us in a full and accessible way.

To be a Christian also means welcoming God into the heart of our life, by allowing his Holy

Spirit to dwell within us and to fill us with his love. This will take a lifetime to happen, during which our relationship with God will become stronger and closer.

The passage goes on to tell us that Christians come to know God's love towards them, and they put their trust in him. We have to believe in Jesus and act on that belief, just as his disciples did in the Gospels. In this way belief becomes active trust, as it does in any other good friendship. The heart of being a Christian is love – our love towards God, and his love towards us. 'God is love; he who dwells in love is dwelling in God, and God in him.'

We should respect God, but we do not need to be afraid of him – he is our Father, and if we want to know what he is like, we can see him in Jesus. We are called day by day to become more like him, as we sense his presence in our hearts.

---

### Pause for reflection

*What is it that attracts me to Jesus?*

*Do I want God to share my life?*

*Am I prepared to become more loving?*

## What Is a Christian?

In the Confirmation service, the bishop will say: 'God has called you by name and made you his own.' What does this mean? The Bible tells us about many people who were called to be the friends and servants of God – for example, Abraham, Moses, Samuel, Elijah, John the Baptist and, most important of all, Jesus himself, as God's son. This sense of being called by God has continued throughout the history of Christianity. From it we get the idea of 'vocation', which simply means an inner sense that God is calling us to love and follow him in all that we do, and that he has a purpose for our lives. When we come to Confirmation we are therefore saying 'Yes' to God's call to us.

What is it that God calls us to be? First, we are called to be children of God. This gives a great purpose and sense of security to our lives. God truly loves us and will never let us down. How can we respond to that love? We are called to be kind and loving people – generous compassion is the key characteristic of Christianity. Jesus said, 'Love one another as I have loved you' (John 13:34).

Secondly, Jesus calls us away from all that is evil and destructive, from sin in all its selfish forms. Jesus restores us to an open and trusting relationship with God. The sign of love is the absence of fear: 'In love there is no room for fear, indeed perfect love banishes fear' (1 John 4:18). We are called to show God's own love and kindness towards others, whoever they may be. If we cannot love others whom we can see, how can we love God whom we cannot see?

Finally, we are called to an eternal life with God in heaven – this present life on earth is a preparation for that. By following the example of Jesus and letting his Spirit fill and guide our lives, we gradually become more like God. The more we are like him in our faithfulness, forgiveness and love, the more we shall be at home with him in heaven.

---

### Prayer

*Eternal God and Father,*
*you create us by your power*
*and you redeem us by your love:*
*guide and strengthen us by your Holy Spirit,*
*that we may give ourselves in love and service*
*to others and to you;*
*through Jesus Christ our Lord.    Amen.*

*(Alternative Service Book)*

---

# Making Decisions

What has brought you to think about Confirmation? If you look back on your life so far, you may be able to see a pattern of influences which have flowed into your life – parents, teachers, priests, friends. Pause for a moment and thank God for those people.

But in the end, being a Christian has to be your own personal and free choice. So at the start of the service of Baptism and Confirmation, the bishop will ask you: 'Are you ready with your own mouth and from your own heart to affirm your faith in Jesus Christ?' He will ask those who are being baptized a further question just before the moment of their baptism: 'Is this your faith?' Each person has to reply: 'This is my faith.'

How does a person actually become a Christian? The Baptism and Confirmation service says: 'In Baptism, God calls us out of darkness into his marvellous light. To follow Christ means dying to sin and rising to new life in him.' To move towards the light of God's love is to turn our backs on all that is evil and sinful – the darkness that can so damage human life. You cannot face two ways at once!

The decision to be confirmed is like picking up a compass that will guide us throughout our journey towards God. Its needle points at all times towards Christ: like the magnetic pole, he draws us to himself. Will we always follow where the needle points? Such moments of decision will come again and again in life. Confirmation is therefore the moment when we decide to wear this compass round our necks and to use it for the rest of our lives.

If we are crossing a mountain and ignore our compass we may get lost. But a compass must be used with a map. In Christianity, this map is found in the Bible, and also in the lives of other Christians, who are sometimes called saints. In the lives of others who have followed God's call, we can see how, in different and often difficult situations, they tried to follow him. Every part of the Bible points to God's truth about himself revealed in Jesus – so the compass and the map work together.

**Pause for reflection**

*Do I turn to Christ?*

*Do I repent of my sins?*

*Do I reject what is evil?*

The questions you will be asked at Confirmation recall the opening pages of the Bible (Genesis chapter 3), where Adam and Eve made fatal choices in the Garden of Eden, and so disobeyed God:

- Do you reject the devil and all rebellion against God?
- Do you renounce the deceit and corruption of evil?
- Do you repent of the sins that separate us from God and neighbour?

Evil is a tragic reality which is destructive and hostile towards us. In human history we have seen it take dreadful forms in war, concentration camps, apartheid, poverty and the abuse of human rights. It damages our personal relationships too, in child abuse, violence, unfaithfulness in marriage, bullying at school and in the workplace, and in many other ways.

It is also very easy to be deceived – for example, by manipulative advertising, by religious or political cults, by other people to whom we feel attracted, and even by ourselves. Evil can take very subtle and attractive forms, but it will always lure us away from God and will in the end turn us against our fellow human beings. Alcoholism and drug abuse are terrible examples of how people can be destroyed while being deceived into thinking that their pursuit of happiness is harmless.

When we feel under pressure in these ways we can draw strength from the example of Jesus. He also faced real temptations, notably at the beginning of his public ministry (you can read all about them in Matthew chapter 4 or Luke chapter 4). His choices are very significant for us too. He was tempted to use his gifts and powers to manipulate things and people for his own purposes. He was tempted to seize power and dominate others, or to deceive people by some dramatic display of miraculous power. Even as he faced death on the Cross he was still being tempted to save himself.

---

**Pause for reflection**

*What temptations do I find hard to resist?*

*How am I going to react to people who pressurize me to do wrong things?*

*Who can I turn to for help?*

---

Jesus chose to serve others, to relate to them freely and lovingly, and not to pressurize them. His power was the power of God's love and forgiveness, and he persuaded people by his own example and teaching. In doing so he showed them how God really looks at human beings and values them. We should do the same, because Christianity teaches us to be honest with ourselves before God, and not to hide or pretend. It enables us to become truly free, able to make rational and loving decisions, and to build sound relationships with others. In the end, how we relate to others is the practical test of how

Christian we are becoming. But we need God's daily help in this.

---

**Prayer**

*O God, without your help we cannot
please you:
mercifully grant that your Holy Spirit
may in all things direct our minds and rule
our hearts,
through Jesus Christ our Lord.
Amen.*

*(Book of Common Prayer)*

---

# Born of Water and the Spirit

Jesus said, 'No one can enter the kingdom of God without being born of water and the Spirit' (John 3:5). What did he mean? Baptism and Confirmation are two parts of the same sacrament, and among the early Christians they were not separated in time. People were baptized and confirmed during a solemn ceremony on the eve of Easter, often after a long preparation. The modern prayer over the water of Baptism unfolds the meaning of these strange words – 'being born of water and the Spirit'.

## Life

*Almighty God, whose Son Jesus Christ was baptized in the river Jordan, we thank you for the gift of water to cleanse and revive us.*

Without water there can be no life. Our human bodies are largely made up of water, and without a water supply human society would collapse. In its description of the creation of the world the Book of Genesis says the Spirit of God hovered over the formless waters and created life within them. Baptism links God's work as the Creator of the world with Jesus' work of re-creating human life. When he was baptized in the river Jordan, Jesus identified himself with human beings in all their weakness and suffering. The Gospels record that he rescued many people from what was destroying their lives and made them whole.

## Freedom

*We thank you that through the waters of the Red Sea you led your people out of slavery to freedom in the promised land.*

Christianity is rooted in history – the history of Jesus and his own people, the Jews. In the Exodus, God revealed his care for his people Israel and rescued them from slavery and geno-cide in Egypt. By leading them to freedom in this way, God made his opposition to cruelty, oppression and evil quite clear. Jesus confirmed this when he said, 'I have come that people may have life in all its fullness' (John 10:10). Faith in Jesus leads us to this fullness of life; and Baptism marks the passing over from an old life to a new one of freedom within the family of God, the Church. Freedom is the hallmark of eternal life, because there is no true love without freedom – freedom from sin and evil, and freedom to love God and to love others as he loves them.

## Light

*We thank you that through the deep waters of death you brought your Son, and raised him to life in triumph.*

Baptism commemorates the death and resurrection of Jesus. Water may give life, but it can also drown. Jesus had first to descend into the darkness of suffering and death, caused by human sin and evil. But by the power of God, the Cross – the place of dark destruction – became the place of light, of new and eternal life. This is the great miracle, the light at the heart of Christianity. The true hope for all human beings is that no evil is too great to be conquered by God's love and power.

## Love

> *Bless this water, that your servants who are washed in it may be made one with Christ in his death and resurrection, to be cleansed and delivered from all sin.*

In Baptism we pray that this eternal miracle of God's re-creating love may touch our lives and begin to change them. We offer ourselves to him in love so that we may escape all that is evil and destructive, and be healed from anything that has damaged our lives. We pray that we may follow Christ closely day by day, and so become more like him. We pray that his Spirit may come into the heart of our lives, so that we may begin to experience a new depth and quality of existence that is a foretaste of eternal life.

> *Send your Holy Spirit upon us, to bring us to new birth in the household of faith, and raise us with Christ to full and eternal life; for all might, majesty, authority and power are yours, now and forever.*

These words of Confirmation seal us with the gift

of the Holy Spirit. They express our willingness to welcome his activity in our lives – an activity which began in a hidden way at Baptism. These words remind us also that there is an eternal life beyond this life. Just as life in the womb prepares us for life in this world, so our life now prepares us for eternal life, which is already flowing into us by the presence of the Holy Spirit.

---

### Prayer

Here is a prayer that we can use each day to ask for the help of God's Spirit:

*Heavenly Father, by the power of your Holy Spirit*
*you give us new life through faith in Jesus expressed in Baptism and Confirmation.*
*Guide and strengthen us by your Spirit that we may serve you and other people in faith and love,*
*through Jesus Christ our Lord.*
*Amen.*

*(Confirmation Service)*

---

# The Gift of the Spirit

When you come to be confirmed it is as if you are offering the lit candle of your own Christian life and faith to God, who in the person of the bishop will then place it in a great candelabra – the Church. Each person has their own particular place in which to shine, and there are many diverging branches to the one candelabra. On its own, your faith might seem flickering and weak, but joined to that of other Christians it will shine forth, communicating God's love to the world. (A more dynamic way of portraying this is to think of a fire made of glowing coals. They glow when they are together, but if separated they just smoulder until they go out!)

A candle is a good symbol of what it means to be a Christian. A candle is made of very simple ingredients – some wax and a string wick. But it can support a flickering flame of light, to which, in the end, it gives the whole of its being. To be a

## The Gift of the Spirit

Christian is to accept the light of God's Spirit at the heart of our life.

---

### Prayer

Here is a simple prayer to remind us of this:

*Come, Holy Spirit,*
*fill now the hearts of your faithful people;*
*and kindle in us the fire of your love.*
*Amen.*

*(Traditional)*

---

Christians believe that God's Spirit comes into the heart of our life at Baptism. Like a seed, his presence grows and influences us until we feel ready to go forward to Confirmation. It is as if God has a hidden trap-door into our heart, while we control the front door of our life, and decide our final response. God cannot force us to love him, but, as St John pointed out, 'we love him because he loved us first' (1 John 4:19). We call this God's 'grace'.

The gift of the Holy Spirit is the miracle at the heart of Christianity. He makes Jesus real to us in a loving and personal way. His presence helps the development of our personality and character. We believe that human beings were made originally 'in the image and likeness of God' (Genesis 1:26). This means that we are designed to be able to receive God's presence at the heart of our lives.

Think now of an elaborate lantern, made of silver and gold, glass and enamel. It is a precious work of art, but until it is filled by the living light of a flame, it is a dead thing. The light transforms it and reveals its true beauty, and it, in turn, throws the light in a unique and wonderful way. This is a picture of our life with God: this explains why we are each made in a unique way, to radiate something true about God.

---

### Prayer

Here is another lovely prayer to the
Holy Spirit which expresses this:

*Grant us your light, O Lord,*
*that the darkness in our hearts being fully*
*passed away,*
*we may come at last to the light*
*which is Christ.   Amen.*

*(Traditional)*

---

## The Gift of the Spirit

This prayer reminds us that there is darkness in our lives that needs to be cleared away – the lantern of our life is often tarnished or bent by sin. God's Spirit comes into our lives to restore what is damaged and to heal what is hurt. He will affect the way we live – he will shape our attitudes and values. As St Paul said: 'the fruit of God's Spirit is love, joy, peace, patience, kindness and self-control' (Galatians 5:22–23).

---

**Pause for reflection**

*Do I truly want to open my heart to God's Spirit?*

*Am I willing to change some of my wrong attitudes?*

*Is there something in my life which needs to be healed by God?*

---

We seek the presence of God's Spirit in our hearts when we pray. St Paul says we are called to become 'the sanctuary of God's Spirit' (1 Corinthians 6:19). Jesus says we are meant to worship God 'in Spirit and in truth' (John 4:23).

The closer we come to God in this way, the closer he will come to us. A life of prayer leads to a life of 'holiness'.

What is 'holiness'? It means a continual sense of God's love for us and protection of us – an awareness that all that we do has a purpose, and that our life is in active partnership with him. In time, people may be able to detect this quality of holiness in us; they may see something of Jesus in our character, attitudes and responses. A holy person makes God seem close and real. As the light of God's Spirit fills every part of our lives, so he is able to shine out from us to attract others to him, and to heal their lives. We call such a person a 'saint'.

This path of holiness begins at Confirmation when the bishop confirms each individual person with the words: 'Confirm, O Lord, your servant with your Holy Spirit.' Just before he does this he prays, using words drawn from the Old Testament (see Isaiah 11:2–3):

*Almighty and ever-living God, you have given your servants new birth by water and the Spirit, and have forgiven them all their sins. Let your Holy Spirit rest upon them: the Spirit of wisdom and understanding, the Spirit of counsel and strength, the Spirit of knowledge and true godliness; and let their delight be in the fear of the Lord.*

The bishop may then mark each person with the sign of the Cross in holy oil that has been especially blessed for this purpose on Maundy Thursday. This is a symbol of being a Christian: the oil represents the anointing of God's Spirit to heal and bless our lives. But we receive this gift only through the suffering, death and resurrection of Jesus. He too was anointed by God's Spirit at his Baptism, and so he is called 'Christ', which means 'God's Anointed One'.

Let us remember his words: 'If anyone is thirsty, let him come to me and drink. Whoever believes in me, as Scripture says, "Streams of living water shall flow from within him"' (John 7:37–38). This is the inner miracle of Christianity – the spring of living water within us which is God's Spirit in our hearts – or, as St Paul put it, 'Christ in you, the hope of glory'.

Water and fire thus both represent to us the mysterious truth of the Holy Spirit affecting our lives.

### Prayer

Here is an ancient and lovely prayer to the Holy Spirit which we can use each day:

*Come, Holy Spirit, our souls inspire,*
*and kindle with celestial fire;*
*thou the anointing Spirit art*
*who dost thy sevenfold gifts impart.*

*Thy blessed unction from above,*
*is comfort, life and fire of love;*
*enable with perpetual light*
*the dullness of our blinded sight.*

*Anoint and cheer our soiled face*
*with the abundance of thy grace;*
*drive far our foes, give peace at home,*
*where thou art guide no ill can come.*

*Teach us to know the Father, Son*
*and Thee, of both, to be but One;*
*that through the ages all along*
*this may be our endless song:*
*praise to thy eternal merit –*
*Father, Son and Holy Spirit.    Amen.*

*(A translation of a medieval Latin hymn)*

PART TWO

# Being a Christian

# Learning to Pray

It is natural for human beings to pray and to worship God. You can see evidence of this in archaeological remains and cultural traditions around the world. Christians believe that the worship of God is the supreme goal of human life. A great Christian theologian, St Augustine, put it this way: 'God has made us for himself, and our hearts are restless until they find their rest in him.' Jesus said that those who truly seek to worship God must do so in spirit and in truth. So how do Christians approach God in private prayer and public worship? The word ACTS can help us to think about this.

## A – Adoration

It is extraordinary to believe that the God who made the universe can be personally known in Jesus. Our natural response is Adoration. We see more and more of God's intelligence and power through modern scientific understanding of how the world was made. But if we ask why this is so, what is the ultimate purpose of our life in this world, we pass into the area of belief.

There need be no conflict between science and belief if we remember that science bases its understanding of how things are upon repeated examination and experiment. Theology, which expresses belief, rests upon an intelligent faith put to the test through prayer, thought and experience stretching back over many centuries of history. One of the greatest Christian philosophers, St Anselm, put it this way: 'Faith seeks understanding.'

We can sense God's intelligence and beauty also through the arts and music. Genesis chapter 1 says that God saw that the world he had made was 'very good'. We can think of God as a master craftsman who created an elaborate musical instrument out of many different materials, and then he expressed himself by playing music on it. Human beings, made 'in the image and likeness of God', are designed to be able to hear and respond to this music. As many artists, poets and musicians have discovered, the world becomes a mirror of God's own beauty.

---

### Point for reflection

*When I consider your heavens –
the work of your fingers . . .
what is man that you should be mindful
of him,
or the son of man that you should care
for him?*

*(Psalm 8:4–5)*

---

## C – Confession

Ours is a flawed world, where human beings often do great damage to each other and to nature. This is our tragedy; we cannot escape it, and it often makes it hard for us to approach God with any confidence. His compassion revealed in Jesus challenges and attracts us, but we often need to sense God's forgiveness first. We have to use the time ahead as an opportunity to put things right. In the New Testament this is called 'repentance' – a change of heart and mind.

In public and in private, as we approach God, we need to recognize the truth of what St Paul said: 'all have sinned and fall short of God's glory' (Romans 3:23). If we ever feel deeply troubled by what we have done, we should go to a priest whom we trust and make a full and private confession to him or her. Through this sacrament of Confession God will touch and heal our lives, and assure us that we are still loved and forgiven.

---

### Point for reflection

*Have mercy on me, O God,*
*in your enduring goodness:*
*according to the fullness of your*
*compassion*
*blot out all my offences.*

*(Psalm 51:1)*

---

## T – Thanksgiving

An ancient word for Holy Communion is the 'Eucharist', which means 'thanksgiving'. This word springs from the language of the New Testament. We thank God for creating us in such a wonderful world, and for loving us so much that he gave his only Son, Jesus Christ, to rescue us from our sins. Like the thief dying on the cross beside Jesus, we cry, 'Lord, remember me when you come in your kingdom!' (Luke 23:42).

This spirit of gratitude lies at the heart of Christianity, and it gives us strength and confidence. It reminds us not to take life for granted: everything we have is a gift from God. That is why we should say grace before we eat and give thanks before we go to sleep. This gratitude will give rise to compassion and generosity, which will be expressed in humility and forgiveness towards others. For, as Jesus declared, 'the person who is forgiven most will love most' (Luke 7:47).

---

### Point for reflection

*Your unchanging goodness is better than life itself:*
*therefore my lips shall praise you.*
*I will bless you as long as I live:*
*and in your Name will I lift up my hands on high.*

*(Psalm 63:4–5)*

---

## S – Supplication

Supplication means praying for others in a spirit of intelligent compassion. Having looked upward to God, we now look outwards to the world that he loves, and we begin to see others with his eyes. Our prayers can embrace everyone we know and love, and they can also reach places and people that we may not even directly know.

Through prayer we can reach out in sympathy to many situations about which we would otherwise feel quite powerless. Where we can help others, we should do so generously, but always with prayer for them in our hearts, knowing that only God can meet their deepest needs. We should take to heart these words of Jesus: 'Inasmuch as you did this for one of these my brethren, you did it to me' (Matthew 25:40).

---

### Point for reflection

*Hear my loud crying, O God:*
*and give heed to my prayer.*
*From the ends of the earth*
*I call to you when my heart faints:*
*O set me on the rock that is higher than I!*

*(Psalm 61:1–2)*

---

So we have seen that the word ACTS can help us to think about prayer. Another key word concerning prayer is LOVE. Christian prayer comes to life when it is fired by love. We are called to be self-giving in love for God and in compassion for others. Our ACTS must express our LOVE.

## L – Loving

Our prayer should always be an expression of our love for God. 'God is love' and 'we love him because he first loved us' (1 John 4:19). When we love someone, we want to spend time with them, to express our feelings towards them, and to give them priority time. All our experiences of human love become preparations for this great love of God. In turn, our love for God will influence how we express our various human affections, and how we love and serve other people.

---

### Point for reflection

*O God, you are my God:*
*eagerly will I seek you.*
*My soul thirsts for you, my flesh longs for you:*
*as a dry and thirsty land where no water is.*

*(Psalm 63:1)*

---

## O – Open

When we come into the presence of God we must be open with him. We cannot hide anything anyway, nor should we try to do so. He loves us for the person we are as well as for what we may become with his guidance. He will forgive us if we are truly sorry. But we must realise that an encounter with God may change our lives – it can be a demanding thing to put ourselves into the hands of the living God.

---

### Point for reflection

*O Lord, my heart is not proud . . .*
*but I have calmed and quieted my soul*
*like a weaned child upon its mother's*
*breast . . .*
*trust in the Lord for ever.*

*(Psalm 131:1-3)*

---

## V – Voluntary

We have to want to pray – it must not be simply a duty laid upon us. We need to organize our prayers and set aside time for them each day. Is praying important to us, or is it something that is squeezed in at the edges of our life? Do we pray regularly, or only when we are in trouble? We will not always feel like praying, and this is when an organized pattern of prayer can help. Consider how important it is to keep in regular touch with your parents and friends – the same is true with God.

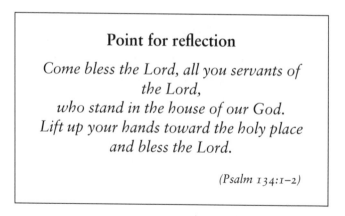

### Point for reflection

*Come bless the Lord, all you servants of the Lord,*
*who stand in the house of our God.*
*Lift up your hands toward the holy place and bless the Lord.*

*(Psalm 134:1–2)*

## E – Expectant

We must pay God full attention if we can. This is
hard, and we are often distracted. But if we work
at prayer we shall find that we have an 'inner ear'
by which we sense God's presence. Meanwhile
you can turn your distractions into short prayers.
If something is worrying you, share it with God.
If you think of someone, pray for them.

Prayer is a great act of faith, and of patience
too, but we must persist in prayer. Often our
waiting for an answer to our prayers gives God
the opportunity to test our hearts and motives.
Any relationship will be unbalanced if one person
does all the talking. We have to learn to sit still
and listen for God, and he will respond in his own
good time. Praying is an art that needs a whole
lifetime of practice. In the end it will become as
natural to us as our breathing.

---

### Point for reflection

*The Lord preserves the simple;*
*when I was brought low he saved me . . .*
*I will walk before the Lord*
*in the land of the living.*

*(Psalm 116:6, 9)*

---

## Planning a prayer life

Praying is an art that we learn through experience. As life moves on, our needs will change, and there will always be something new to learn about how to pray. Here are some practical steps to help you to establish your own prayer life:

- Set aside some time each day for your prayers – start with just five minutes. Find somewhere quiet and private to pray – perhaps outdoors in good weather.

- Put together a balanced pattern of prayers – some of them should be written down and traditional, while others should be personal and spontaneous. Leave time to be quiet in the presence of God as well. Remember to pray for others in a regular and caring way.

- Find some spiritual reading in addition to the Bible: let someone else's experience teach and guide you. Keep such a book on the go, and read it twice a week at least.

- Pray as you travel to school, college or work; pray briefly in the midst of your work. Pray with your family; and don't be afraid to pray with someone in trouble if they ask you to do so.

- Don't rush into church or chatter aimlessly before a service! Make time to prepare for worship, perhaps by reading through parts of the service in advance, or by looking at the Bible readings for the day. In church, remember that you are there to give as well as to receive.

- Find someone you can trust – a Christian friend, or perhaps a priest, a monk or a nun – who will listen to you, pray for you and guide you further in your prayers. Try not to become isolated in your Christian life.

# Reading the Bible

Christianity is built upon Jesus Christ, and he is revealed to us through the Gospels. The backdrop to the Gospels is the Old Testament, which Jews and Muslims also regard as a holy book. The meaning of the Gospels is explained by the rest of the New Testament, which was written by the Apostles Peter, James, John and Paul and a few other members of the early Church. The Bible is called 'the Word of God' because it speaks about Jesus, who is God's Word (see John 1:1).

We need to make time to read the Bible in an intelligent and prayerful way. Some people find it helpful to study sections of the Bible, day by day, with the assistance of Bible-reading notes. Others focus on the Sunday readings, found in the Prayer Book or a lectionary. There are also many attractive commentaries available which will further unlock the meaning of the Bible.

If we look at the pattern of readings at Holy Communion we can sometimes see helpful connections between the different parts of the Bible. For example, if the Gospel reading were the Feeding of the Five Thousand (see Mark chapter 6), the Old Testament reading might come from the Exodus story of the manna in the desert (see Exodus chapter 16), and the Psalm might be 'The Lord is my Shepherd' (Psalm 23). There might be a passage from another part of the New Testament explaining the significance of the Gospel – for example, St Paul writing about the Eucharist to the church at Corinth (1 Corinthians chapter 11). This kind of connection is often reflected in Christian works of art.

---

**Points for reflection when reading the Bible**

*What is this passage telling me about God or Jesus?*

*What is it telling me about how I should treat others?*

*What is it telling me about how I should approach God in prayer?*

---

Christians believe that the mind behind the Bible is the mind of God, seeking to communicate to human beings throughout history. There is therefore a consistent pattern and purpose running through the Bible, even though it was written by many different people over many centuries. When we read the Bible, we should pray that God's Spirit will make a bit of this pattern clear and relevant to us today.

At one level, the Bible in a good modern translation is readily accessible to any reader. But at another level, it is a complex body of writing, originally in Hebrew and Greek, and composed by many different people. That is why the Bible has become one of the most studied books from the ancient world. Some parts are easier to understand than others, and there are a few parts that may almost put us off altogether!

For Christians, the Gospels are the most accessible part of the Bible, and it a good idea to read part of a Gospel each day, or at least several times a week. They give us different angles on Jesus and his teaching. The first three Gospels (Matthew, Mark and Luke) have a close family connection, but with subtle variations of emphasis. John's Gospel stands a bit apart, but it often helps us to understand the meaning of the other three Gospels.

The rest of the New Testament is dominated by the writings of St Paul. He was converted to Christianity, having for a while persecuted Christians. The book called 'Acts' describes this, and gives a vivid picture of the growth of the early Church throughout the Roman world. Paul himself experienced the turmoil that many Jews were going through at that time, as they adjusted to this new belief about Jesus, with its challenge of being open to those who were not Jews (called Gentiles). His letters contain much practical guidance about how to live as a Christian, as well as explanations of different aspects of belief about Jesus.

The Old Testament is sometimes more difficult to understand, and parts of it seem very remote indeed. Perhaps the Psalms are the best way into the spirit and message of the Old Testament. It has been the custom of the Church since the earliest times to use the Psalms regularly in public worship and private prayer. Christians place the life and suffering of Jesus as a kind of filter over the Old Testament, because we believe that it is in Jesus' personality that God has most fully revealed himself. As a result, some parts of the Old Testament come to life in an extraordinary way. For example, if you read Isaiah chapter 53 you find a picture of the meaning of suffering that seems to point directly to what happened to Jesus. On the other hand, what happened to him may equally block out certain things that are said about God, removing some of the gory and bloodthirsty bits to the safety of history! Christians have to remember that 'God is Christ-like, and in him is nothing unlike Christ at all' (William Temple).

---

### Prayer

*Almighty God,*
*we thank you for the gift*
*of your holy word.*
*May it be a lantern to our feet,*
*a light to our paths,*
*and a strength to our lives.*
*Take us and use us*
*to love and serve others*
*in the power of the Holy Spirit,*
*and in the Name of your Son,*
*Jesus Christ our Lord.    Amen.*

*(Alternative Service Book)*

---

# Being a Christian Today

Christians inherit from the Old Testament the Ten Commandments (see Exodus 20:1–17) as the basic framework of ethics. The word 'ethics' means those principles which guide how we should behave. The Ten Commandments were commended by Jesus, who added to them the important new commandments of the gospel: 'Love your enemies' and 'Love one another as I have loved you.' Christians are therefore called to love God with all their heart and mind and strength, and to love others with the kind of love that Jesus showed. This takes a lifetime of learning! What do the Ten Commandments, seen in the light of the teaching and example of Jesus, mean for us today?

- We worship only one God (and we share this belief with Jews and Muslims); but he is revealed to us in Jesus, and made real to us by the Holy Spirit.

- We should not allow any thing, or any political belief, or any person to become the focus of our loyalty or desire in a way which would crowd out God, or undermine our relationship with him. If we have a crucifix or icon we do not worship it as an image: it is more like a photograph to call to mind someone whom we love and wish to remember.

- We should not use the Name of God as a swear word. We should not commit perjury (i.e. tell lies) in court. We should also respect how the followers of other religions feel about their names for God.

- We should keep Sunday as a special day for worship in church and recreation with our family. By doing this we remember each week the resurrection of Jesus, and the importance of setting time aside for God each day.

- We should value and respect our parents, and we should build up family life in every way.

- We should never murder anyone – either literally or by our attitudes, words, hatred or jealousy.

- We should not undermine marriage by sexual unfaithfulness or cruelty; nor should we engage in sexual relationships before or outside marriage. Our bodies are to be dwelling-places of the Holy Spirit.

- We must not steal, remembering that honesty builds trust within relationships.

- We must not tell lies or blacken anyone's character: lying destroys relationships.

- We should not covet things that belong to other people, nor should we be jealous of them. The Book of Genesis tells us that jealousy was part of the downfall of the first human beings and the root of many destructive acts.

By his teaching and example Jesus shows us that we should have a positive and kind attitude towards other people, based on forgiveness, truthfulness and trust. We should follow Jesus in being self-sacrificing and generous, serving other people and showing them God's compassion. Jesus himself said: 'The Son of Man did not come to be served, but to serve, and to give up his life as a ransom for many' (Mark 10:45). In this way we

shall truly become ambassadors for Christ – at
school, at home, or at work.

---

### Prayer

Here is a prayer to help us to do
this each day:

*Remember, O Lord, what you have
begun in us,
and not what we deserve:
and as you have called us to your service,
make us worthy of that calling;
through Jesus Christ our Lord.
Amen.*

*(St Leo the Great)*

---

Becoming a Christian leads to a gradual but
deep change of attitude towards others, and to
realising that certain values, derived from the Ten
Commandments and the teaching of Jesus, are
supremely important for human society. In some
parts of the world, belief in these values may
mark a person out for persecution and suffering.

Even in Britain, being a Christian may mean that a person is unable to support a policy at work that they know to be dishonest. They may have to stand up against bullying and discrimination at school or in the workplace. What are the most important Christian values?

## Freedom

We believe that God created us free, and that Jesus died to restore to human beings the capacity to be free. God cannot force us to be good or loving: it is our choice. We believe, however, that everyone has the right to be free in a lawful way: free from poverty, discrimination and cruelty; free to express themselves, to work and to travel, to create, to think, to write and to worship. We call these 'human rights', and for Christians their root lies in the teachings and actions of Jesus in the Gospels. In the words of Jesus: 'If the Son sets you free, you will indeed be free' (John 8:36). That is why Christians resist addiction to alcohol and drugs, as these undermine human personality and freedom.

## Justice

If people are oppressed by poverty and neglect, or condemned to poor housing, health-care and education, they can hardly begin to live the 'life in all its fullness' (John 10:10) that Jesus came to bring. He showed this in the Gospels by his compassion for the poor. In many countries of the world, Christians take the lead in challenging and overcoming such social injustice. Christianity proclaims the possibility of forgiveness and reconciliation between different groups of people who have been in conflict. But this can only occur on the basis of justice and truth. Differences between people allow them to develop fully and to express themselves, and these differences should be respected and valued. But differences should not create or be used to justify inequality of opportunity or social divisions, which might breed hostility and violence.

## Possessions

Christians have to try and disentangle in their minds what they need from what they want. This is not at all easy in modern Western society, where people are bombarded by advertisements making them wish they had more. Yet it is a shocking fact that our kind of society is using up a vast amount of the world's natural resources in a way that poorer countries can never hope to match. We are in danger of being possessed by our possessions, of becoming too dependent on being able to fulfil our immediate desires. Jesus said that 'Man is not to live on bread alone, but on every word that comes from the mouth of God' (Matthew 4:4). We must not lose our willingness or our freedom to give generously to those in need at home or abroad, or to make sacrifices in our way of life in order to follow Jesus more closely.

## Respect

'God so loved the world that he gave his only Son, that whoever believes in him should not perish but have eternal life' (John 3:16). This famous summary of the gospel shows that each human person is of unique value to God, and therefore we should value each equally too. To be able to do this is one of the goals of the Christian life. This means that Christians value the 'sanctity of human life' from the moment of its natural conception in the womb until the moment of natural death. Christianity therefore opposes the use of torture, capital punishment and euthanasia, and the widespread use of abortion. Christians have a special duty to contribute to the education of the young and the care of the sick, the handicapped and the elderly. We are called to love others as we would wish to be loved ourselves. We should show courtesy, hospitality and toleration to others, whatever their racial, religious or social background, and we should treat everyone as being of equal worth to God, and therefore to us as well.

## Sexuality

Christianity places a very high value on human sexuality. It is the means of creating future human lives within the secure environment which is to be found in a lifelong and loving relationship between a man and a woman in marriage. This has been a central part of Christian teaching since the time of the New Testament. Nothing should happen before or during marriage which might undermine the chances of such a stable and life-giving relationship occurring, because children depend on security and love for their well-being. Unfaithfulness and cruelty are enemies of family life.

Sexual relationships before or outside marriage are not compatible with Christian belief and practice. In their obedience to this belief Christians have often found themselves in a minority in society, in the past and certainly today. When we find ourselves under pressure to conform to very different attitudes among our friends in this matter, we need to remember that being a Christian involves respecting God's will for us and others, in the confidence that he only desires what will be best for our lives and personalities.

St Paul teaches that our bodies become 'sanctuaries' in which the Holy Spirit comes to dwell. They are integral to our personalities, and how we treat them matters greatly. As Christians we are called to offer all of ourselves as a 'living sacrifice' to God. For some people, this may mean that they never marry, but remain celibate in obedience and service to God. For others it means that the desire to love and obey God results in chastity – the restricting of sexual activity to marriage, out of respect for God's will that human sexuality should never be separated from its life-giving and loving purpose for both children and parents. If we seek God's help to obey him in this important area of our lives, we shall discover what is best for us and for those we love most. In practical terms, we should never engage in sexual activity which is unloving and uncommitted – or unprotected by contraception, unless children are thoughtfully desired.

## Compassion

Love runs like a golden thread throughout Christianity. We believe that it springs from God himself, for, in the words of St John, 'God is love' (1 John 4:8). In a dramatic parable, Jesus showed that at the end of their lives, human beings will be judged by God on the sole basis of the compassion that they have shown to others in need: 'Anything you did for one of my brothers here, however insignificant, you did for me' (Matthew 25:40). The point is that our love expresses our belief – about God and about other people. The regular giving of money and aid to charities is an important sign of our practical commitment to compassion. So too is our willingness to consider working in one of the caring professions – medicine, nursing, social work, teaching, or the Church's ministry.

These values are common to all human beings and societies – they are not a Christian monopoly. Wherever they are found, they are to be encouraged and valued, whether people call themselves Christians or not. But when they are under pressure, Christians know that they are underpinned by God's own love towards human beings, revealed in the life and death of Jesus. Like him, Christians may sometimes have to be willing to suffer and even to die in defence of these beliefs and values, knowing that if they do so, they are securing the very foundations of human society – its freedom and its true welfare.

# Spiritual Growth

St Paul described the Christian life as a race, for which we need to prepare fully. Another, older idea in the Bible is that of a pilgrimage to the promised land of God's eternal kingdom. Many of the parables of Jesus use pictures of seeds and growth. All these images communicate the idea that being a Christian is a lifelong development and preparation. Just as an athlete must train steadily and single-mindedly, or an artist or musician must strenuously practise his or her skills, so Christians must devote time, energy and self-discipline to the development of their spiritual life in response to the various changes and demands of life. As St Bernard, who lived in the Middle Ages, once said: 'Life is given us so that we may learn how to love: time is given that we may find God.'

How is this done? A regular habit of prayer and Bible reading at home and going to church for Holy Communion each week, if possible, is the foundation. We have to make these commitments an absolute priority at the heart of our life. It is often a help also to go to a regular Christian group meeting to study the Bible and to pray together. It is important to find sympathetic Christian friends, and to be able to talk with your priest or another experienced person in your local church. You cannot develop fully as a Christian in isolation, and sometimes you will need the support and encouragement of others.

Spiritual reading is important too as a complement to the Bible. Today it is possible to obtain valuable writings by Christians of the past from many different branches of the Church. Becoming familiar with the life and thought of great Christians – like St Anselm, who was Archbishop of Canterbury in the Middle Ages, or St Francis of Assisi, who died in the thirteenth century but whose influence still persists today – can teach us a great deal about what it means to know God and to be a Christian. It is inspiring to feel part of a great and living tradition of faith, and to be able to draw on the experience of the past when facing problems today.

Visiting other Christian churches at home or abroad can also enrich our own vision and spiritual life. It is also important to welcome Christian visitors from abroad or from other branches of the Christian Church – hospitality can be a blessing to both the giver and the receiver. Often by such visits and encounters some new aspect of Christianity will suddenly spring to life and leave a lasting impression. This will help us to pray for other parts of the Church and to sustain the new friendships that have been made. Pilgrimage to some great historic centre of our faith, like Rome or Canterbury, can help us to sense the living nature of the Church through history. It may also touch us deeply to pray at concentration camp sites in Europe, Asia or Russia where people have died for their faith.

### Pause for reflection

*Have I organized my life so that I can pray regularly?*
*How strong is my link with my local church?*
*Can I find some way of connecting with the wider Church?*

Going on retreat at a monastery or convent or attending a weekend of teaching and fellowship at a Christian conference centre can help us to build up our spiritual life. Many people find it valuable to spend some time each year in quiet and reflection in such a place. Retreats can either be guided by someone or else completely private – perhaps even silent. This is time spent in the presence of God, away from our normal activities and preoccupations. Offered sincerely to him, such a time will not leave our life untouched. If your job involves dealing with people and their needs, such a time of spiritual renewal may be vital, since you cannot give out to others unless you also receive strength from God.

If you enjoy art or music, then familiarity with great works of Christian art and music will probably deepen and strengthen your spiritual life. If you work in a city and can find time in a lunch-hour to slip into a church or cathedral, perhaps for a brief service, you will be able to sense more strongly the presence and love of God at the heart of all you do. Sensitivity to Christian art, music or poetry may help us to express our own hopes and feelings, and may equip us to respond more fully to hidden aspects of Christianity in different human cultures.

Having a spiritual director is another way of being guided in the Christian life of prayer. A priest or a member of a religious community (a monk or a nun) may be able to provide us with stable, detached but compassionate guidance and encouragement. If there are things in our lives or our past that trouble our conscience or seem to be a barrier between ourselves and God, then making a full and formal confession to a priest, which will be heard in the strictest confidence, may be a way forward. The priest can reassure us of God's love and forgiveness for us, and can offer some sympathetic guidance. The knowledge that there is someone in the background of our lives who knows us in this way and to whom we are in some sense accountable can be very helpful, especially if we feel that we are without a sense of direction or are running into personal problems.

Being a Christian is a lifelong journey towards God and his eternal kingdom. If we offer our lives to him at the start of each day, all that happens to us can have meaning, value and purpose, even if it involves suffering and disappointment. Jesus said: 'Set your mind on God's kingdom and his justice before everything else, and all the rest will come to you as well' (Matthew 6:33). Or in words of wisdom from the Old Testament: 'Put all your trust in the Lord, and do not rely on your own understanding. At every step you take keep him in mind, and he will direct your paths' (Proverbs 3:5–6). We must therefore actively and patiently seek God's will for our lives, and then accept it cheerfully. When we look back over a year, we should then be able to see something of the path we have travelled, and to appreciate what we have learned about God and about others as our experience and understanding of Christianity have grown and unfolded.

---

### Prayer

*Teach us, good Lord,*
*to serve Thee as Thou deservest:*
*to give and not to count the cost;*
*to fight and not to heed the wounds;*
*to labour and not to ask for any reward,*
*except that of knowing that we do Thy will,*
*O Lord, our helper and redeemer.*
*Amen.*

*(St Ignatius Loyola)*

---

# PART THREE

# Belonging to the Church

# What Do Christians Believe?

Christian belief is summed up in the Creeds of the Church. The oldest of these was written in Rome in about AD 200, when Christians were being killed for their faith. It is called the Apostles' Creed, and it sums up the message of the New Testament. It is often said at Morning and Evening Prayer.

The creed used at the Eucharist is called the Nicene Creed. You can find the text of this Creed on page 139. It was drawn up at two meetings of the bishops of the Church – one at Nicaea (in modern Turkey) in AD 325 and one at Constantinople (modern Istanbul) in AD 371. It sets out in more detail Christian belief about Christ and the Holy Spirit.

There are two other creeds, though these are not used in church services. One of them is the statement of the Church Council which met in Chalcedon (also in modern Turkey) in AD 451. It defines more closely how Jesus can be both God and a human person. There is also the later Latin creed (called 'Quicunque vult'), which summarizes Christian belief in Christ and in God as the Trinity of Father, Son and Holy Spirit.

The purpose of the Creeds is to define Christian belief in the language of the New Testament, in a way that can be easily remembered and taught. Outside this pattern of belief, Christians may well lose their way and end up believing in a distorted form of Christianity instead. But if they live and pray within the tradition of the Creeds, they will come to know God as Father, through faith in Jesus Christ, who is made real to them by the gift of the Holy Spirit.

## What we believe about God

We believe in only one God, as do Jews and Muslims: this is called 'monotheism'. But Christians believe that within this one God there are three persons – the Father, the Son and the Holy Spirit. This belief about the nature of God is called faith in 'the Trinity'.

Belief in the Trinity rests upon the teaching and example of Jesus. We believe that he is God's Son; he prayed to God as Father; and he promised the gift of the Holy Spirit. The spiritual experience of

Christians ever since has confirmed the truth of this belief about God.

How can we begin to make sense of this belief? Here is a way of thinking about it: if 'God is Love', as St John teaches (1 John 4:16), then within true love we shall always find the *Giver*, the *Giving* and the *Gift*. God the Father *gives* Jesus the Son and also the Holy Spirit for the life of humanity. The Spirit is *given* to us through the *self-giving* of the Son; and the Son was *given* to his mother, Mary, by the *giving* of the Holy Spirit. 'God so loved the world that he *gave* his only Son, that everyone who has faith in him may not perish but have eternal life' (John 3:16).

God is the Father of Jesus, and he taught us in the Lord's Prayer that we too should call God 'Our Father'. In another sense, God is the Father of all human beings, because the Bible teaches (see Genesis 1:26–27) that we are made in his 'image and likeness'. As Christians we are called to live as children of God, who truly cares for us personally and deeply, as any good parent or friend would do.

God is also the Being who is greater than anything else in existence. As he revealed to Moses in the story of the Burning Bush (see

Exodus 3:1–6), he has always existed. The Bible teaches that God is also the Creator of all that exists in the universe – he made everything that can be seen and measured (e.g. in physics and maths) and also all those things that can only be sensed (e.g. by art or emotion). As an early English saint, Julian of Norwich, once glimpsed, the universe is a very small thing held safely like a tiny nut in the hand of God. Without his loving care there would be nothing at all.

## What we believe about Jesus

Jesus came into human history as the Messiah who had been promised to the Jews in the Old Testament. The word 'Messiah' means 'God's chosen or anointed one' and, translated into Greek, the word becomes 'Christ'. We believe that in the person of Jesus, God became a human being – this belief is called 'the Incarnation'. Jesus comes from God to make him known to us in a full and definitive way. Jesus is the true image and likeness of God. If you want to know how God relates to human beings, you will find out by looking into the person and teaching of Jesus.

In Jesus, God's only Son, God gave himself for

us – suffering and dying on the Cross so that we might know his great love for us. Jesus came into history to rescue us from sin and evil, which destroy mankind. He did this by his teaching and example, by his compassion and miracles, and supremely by his death on the Cross. There, in a deep and mysterious way, by his love and forgiveness, God broke evil's stranglehold over human life. The Cross is the place where the power of God's love triumphs over evil's love of power and cruelty. 'The Son of Man did not come to be served, but to serve, and to give up his life as a ransom for many' (Mark 10:45).

The miracle at the heart of Christianity is the Resurrection. Christians believe, and come to sense, that Jesus is alive and real today, and may be known and loved as well. Even in the darkest place of evil and human suffering, the light of his love shines and can never be put out. The Resurrection of Jesus reveals that 'God became human so that we might come to share in his eternal life' (see 2 Peter 1:3–4). This belief is the key to understanding why the universe exists and how history is unfolding, and it reassures us that God has a purpose for us, as individuals and as the human race. Christ becomes the focal point for understanding all of this, and by the standard of his life and example our own lives will one day be judged by God. How much like Christ shall we become?

## What we believe about the Holy Spirit

The Holy Spirit is God present and active in our lives. We may sense him as we pray and worship, as we show kindness to others, and as we ponder the beauty of the world in nature and art. His life and love gradually change the lives of those who welcome him into their hearts. St Paul said that Christians are called to be the 'sanctuary of the Holy Spirit'. Our human life is like a candle – a small, fragile thing of no great worth in itself, but capable of bearing the living flame of God's invisible love, as we give ourselves to him. Our individual personalities are like many beautiful lanterns with different facets – they only come to life when they are filled with God's light within.

The Holy Spirit is the 'giver of life'. He is the creating power of God, sustaining the life of the universe. He is also the re-creating power of God, restoring human beings until they truly exist 'in the image and likeness of God'. This begins at

Baptism and is renewed at Confirmation, when we pray and when receive Holy Communion.

God's Spirit has spoken through many prophets and saints in the Bible and in Christian history – and through many good and holy people in other faiths too. He is the voice of God's truth and love, challenging evil and recalling human beings to the path of goodness and love. He also speaks through our conscience.

## What we believe about the Church

The Church is the body of all Christians, throughout the world and throughout history. It is *one* in its faith in Jesus Christ, despite a rich diversity of expression in the different Christian churches. It is *holy* because it is the work of God's purpose and love. It is *catholic* in the sense that it is universal – it is for everyone, regardless of race or colour. It is *apostolic* because its roots lie in the witness of the Apostles – those who knew Jesus and who wrote the New Testament.

The Church is founded upon forgiveness and reconciliation. St Peter and St Paul represent this. Both died for their faith in Rome in AD 63 and are buried there – the persecuted and the persecutor.

The gospel of Jesus proclaims God's willingness to forgive all who repent and turn to him. This is made available to us through Baptism.

The Church exists in three ways: in heaven, where all those who have died in Christ experience God's eternal life to which we are all called; in the various local church communities, as they meet to worship; and in the hearts of Christians as they pray.

Eternal life means life with God for ever in the fullness of personal existence. Death is not the end: we believe that the whole person is held in the love of God. So this present life is like a womb preparing us for eternal life. Saints are those Christians who already experience a deep measure of this eternal life, and whose holiness, love and prayers draw others closer to God.

# What Is the Church?

In Confirmation we commit ourselves to be active members of the Church. At the same time the bishop confirms that we belong to the Christian faith and community. The bishop represents several important aspects of the Church. He reminds us that our local church is part of the wider Church – in the diocese, in our country, throughout the Anglican Communion. The bishop also stands for all those who, in every generation, have passed on the Christian faith. In a sense, therefore, the bishop represents Jesus' first Apostles. Finally the bishop reminds us that we have a double loyalty as Christians – to our own particular church, and to the whole Church of God throughout the world.

In the New Testament, there are two pictures of the Church that are particularly important: Jesus used the parable of the vine (John 15:1–10) and St Paul used the analogy of the human body (1 Corinthians 12:12–27). Jesus also told a little parable about the kingdom of God being like a tiny seed which became a vast tree (Mark 4:30–32).

The Tree is a good picture of the unity of the Church: its roots lie deep in the faith of the Jews that is found in the Old Testament. Its seed is the life, death and resurrection of Jesus himself. Its trunk, which supports the entire weight of the tree, is found in the New Testament and the Creeds, which Christians everywhere accept. Its rising sap is the hidden presence of the Holy Spirit, who gives life to every branch, and enables Christians to produce the fruits of God's Spirit (see Galatians 5:22–23) – the signs of his presence within us. The Tree's many branches are the different Christian churches as they have grown up over time, each with its own history and character. They had to grow apart from each other for a while so that the whole shape of the Tree could be expressed, but they are all parts of the one Tree.

The human body is a good picture of the Church in its rich and interdependent diversity. Another way of expressing this would be to think of an orchestra. Different people play different instruments, and everyone has a distinctive and vital part to play in the music, because we all have different gifts and personalities. But the orchestra must keep its eye on the conductor if the music is to be played as it should be. Each musician has to practise hard and continually and must remain in tune. In different periods of history the music will be played in different ways, although it is the same music and the same message. Finally, no orchestra plays just to itself: the Church is called to play the music of God's message of love to each generation of human beings.

---

### Pause for reflection

*What can I contribute to the life of my local church?*

*How can I pray for some other branch of the Church?*

*What special gifts has God given me to develop as a Christian?*

---

Some Christians are called by God to play a leading role within the life of a church. The orchestra needs leaders of its various sections, and it certainly needs a conductor! To such a leader falls the difficult task of understanding the music, holding the orchestra together, listening hard to its playing, and being the focus of its unity.

In the Church there are various types of Christian leaders or ministers. The word 'minister' means 'servant'. This is the foundation of all Christian leadership, following the example of Jesus, who 'did not come to be served but to serve'. The other picture of leadership in the New Testament is that of the shepherd, modelled on Jesus, the Good Shepherd, who laid down his life for the sheep (see John 10:1–18). The word 'pastor' means 'shepherd'.

In the Anglican, Catholic, Orthodox and Lutheran churches there are three 'orders' of ministry: deacons, priests and bishops. The word 'deacon' comes from the New Testament and simply means 'servant'. The word 'priest' means 'elder', someone with the age and experience to lead and teach others. The word 'bishop' means 'overseer', someone who cares for the life of the wider Church and its ministers.

These ordained ministers also remind us that every Christian is called by God to offer their life in love and service to him and to others. There are certain professions which can be forms of Christian ministry too, such as medicine, nursing, social work, teaching and any work which involves the active care of people. Whatever our work may be, it is important that we see it in the light of our duty towards God, and that we care for the people with whom we work, or whom we manage, in a Christian spirit. Where we are – at home, at school, in the workplace – is where we have to discover how to be Christian in the service of others.

Christian marriage is another way of responding to Christ's call to love others as he loves us. A lifelong and loving relationship between a man and a woman has to be built on forgiveness, kindness, loyalty, self-sacrifice, patience and affection. It can be a tough commitment – as can having children! But the responsibility of being a parent – enabling children to flourish as people throughout their lives – can be seen as a way of mirroring God's love for the young. A Christian home can be a powerful expression of the reality of Christianity in any community.

Some people are called to join a religious community as a monk or a nun. This has always been a very important way of being a Christian and of strengthening the life and witness of the Church. This is a lifelong commitment that rules out marriage and family life, and it is not always easy. But religious communities often work in places of poverty and difficulty in the name of Christ; or they can simply be places of prayer, offering support to other Christians in their family life and work. Having friends who are members of a religious community can be a real help in being a Christian.

We sense the life of the wider Church, and its needs and opportunities, when we pray for other Christians at home or abroad. It is important to be well informed about the work of other churches, Christian missions and charitable organizations, to give them money as we can, and to take a genuine interest in them. We should be generous in our compassion for those in other countries who are suffering poverty and persecution, and we should never miss an opportunity to be hospitable to Christians from other churches or from abroad. We should remember the words of St Gregory, who sent the first missionaries to England: 'Your holy deeds are where you are, but your prayers reach where you cannot be.'

### Prayer

*O God of unchangeable power and of
eternal light:
look with favour upon your whole
Church,
that wonderful and sacred mystery;
and by the peaceful operation of your
perpetual providence,
carry out the work of our salvation:
and let the whole world feel and see
that things which had grown old are being
made new,
that things which had decayed are being
restored,
and that all things are returning into unity
in him by whom they were made,
your Son, Jesus Christ our Lord.
Amen.*

*(Gelasian: from early medieval Rome)*

# Time and Eternity:
# The Christian Year

People today often complain that they are so busy and that they have no time! Time for what? How should Christians use their time? How should we understand the nature, meaning and purpose of time?

Being a Christian means living in three time-zones at once. There is normal time – day by day, month by month, year by year. Parallel to this is the Christian calendar of seasons and feasts. Then there is the whole question of how our existence in time relates to and is influenced by God's eternal existence.

One way of thinking about the last question is to consider a wheel. The circumference represents the time-line of human existence through history. We often feel very distant from those who have lived in the past – their lives were so different to ours that they seem to be irrelevant to us. But in a wheel, each point of the circumference is connected to the centre by spokes. If the hub of the wheel, which turns but is always still, represents the eternal existence of God, are there spokes of connection down which we may move by our prayers, and which bring us closer to the centre? If there are, do they also bring us closer to those who, though distant in time, have come close to God? Jesus taught that this is so when he said: 'God is not the God of the dead but of the living: in his sight all are alive' (Luke 20:38). The Christian calendar reminds us of this other dimension to our existence in time – it connects us to God's eternal existence, and prepares us for it.

The Christian year is divided into two halves. From Advent to Pentecost we consider different aspects of the life of Jesus:

- *Advent:* The preparation in the Old Testament for Christ's coming; and the goal of human history as revealed in him – heaven and hell, death and judgement.

- *Christmas:* The Virgin Mary gives birth to Jesus at Bethlehem.

- *Epiphany:* The coming of the wise men; and the Baptism of Jesus by John the Baptist.

- *Lent:* The life and ministry of Jesus; his teaching and miracles; and our following him in preparation for Holy Week and Easter.

- *Holy Week:* The suffering of Jesus in Jerusalem from Palm Sunday to Good Friday, including the giving of the Last Supper on Maundy Thursday.

- *Easter:* The resurrection of Jesus from death.

- *Ascension:* The eternal existence of Jesus in heaven as God's only Son.

- *Pentecost:* The coming of the Holy Spirit and the birth of the Church.

- *Trinity:* God's self-revelation as Father, Son and Holy Spirit.

During the rest of the year after Trinity until Advent, through the set readings in church, we have the opportunity to learn more about the meaning of the life and teaching of Jesus and about God's purpose for human life.

## Time and Eternity

The Christian calendar also commemorates, on different dates through the year, some of the most notable events and saints in Christian history. They remind us that we are part of a living tradition of faith and prayer. You can think of this as a series of concentric rings:

- At the core stand the most important feasts to do with Jesus and his mother Mary: *the Annunciation*, when Mary accepted God's call to bear Jesus; *the Presentation*, when Mary presented Jesus in the Temple; *the Transfiguration*, when Jesus appeared in glory to his disciples.

- There are also festivals for St John the Baptist, the Conversion of St Paul, and for the various Apostles of Jesus.

- Then come the feasts of the martyrs – those who died for their faith.

- Then there are commemorations for a broad band of saints – men and women from across history who have influenced the growth and teaching of the Church in various ways.

- Finally we remember the saints of more modern times, including those who were put to death for being Christians.

The saints who are formally remembered in this way are only a representative sample of all the many Christians who have led holy lives, and so have drawn others to God. Saints are like stars – they shed light back to us, even as they move onwards in heaven towards God. Often they seem to cluster like constellations in different periods of the Church's history.

Our own country has a rich tradition of saints, whose lives shed light on the Christian character of Britain. Their lives encourage us who have inherited the Church they created, and their prayers support us in our own pilgrimage towards the eternal kingdom of God's love. Here are some of the more notable British saints:

- Alban, the first known British martyr in Roman times.
- Patrick, the bishop who took Christianity from Britain to Ireland.
- David, a bishop and monk in Wales.

- Columba, the first abbot of the monastery of Iona in Scotland.

- Gregory, the pope who sent the missionaries to England in 597.

- Augustine, the first archbishop of Canterbury.

- Aidan, an Irish missionary bishop who worked in northern England.

- Cuthbert, the first English saint at Lindisfarne.

- Hilda, an abbess of the monastery of Whitby.

- Bede, the historian of the early English Church.

- Boniface, an English missionary bishop who worked in Germany.

- Dunstan, an archbishop of Canterbury in the tenth century.

- Anselm, a medieval archbishop of Canterbury and a philosopher.

- Hugh, a monk and a bishop of Lincoln in the twelfth century.

- Julian, a female mystic in Norwich in the fourteenth century.

- Thomas More, a statesman and a martyr at the time of the Reformation.

- John Wesley, an evangelist in the eighteenth century.

- William Wilberforce, an anti-slavery campaigner in the nineteenth century.

- Michael Ramsey, an archbishop of Canterbury in the twentieth century.

So how should Christians regard their use of time? Remember the words of St Bernard: 'Life is given that we may learn how to love; time is given that we may find God.' It is all too easy for life to crowd out God, and for 'the barrenness of a busy life to create the busyness of a barren life', so that we end up cut off from a sense of God and of eternal life. That is why, in the Ten Commandments, one day is set aside for rest and the worship of God. Christians obey this commandment by keeping Sunday as a special day. We also need to discipline ourselves to spend time with God in prayer each day.

Social and work pressures can make us too busy to spend time with God, and they can also make us too busy for other people, including our own friends and family. Christians are called to be free men and women, striking a sound balance between the demands of work and leisure, and not valuing money, possessions and careers above their relationships with God and other people. We must not end up being people who pass by others who are in need because we have no time.

Time, like much else, is one of God's gifts to us. That is why starting and ending each day with prayer helps us to remember that all of our time is lived in God's presence and should be devoted to serving him and other people. Our rhythm of prayer and regular worship in church can prevent us from becoming, in the end, too busy for our own good.

# Why Be a Christian?

You must not be surprised if this question occurs to you after Confirmation! Being a Christian is an act of intelligent faith – it does not rule out the hard questions in life. Often people will ask us these questions because they want to know how a Christian approaches them. Christianity does not offer easy or complete answers to all the issues that trouble human beings. But 'faith seeks understanding', so it is important that we should think about how we might respond to some of the difficult questions that our friends may ask us.

## If God exists, what is he like, and how do we know about him?

Christians believe that God exists because the intricacy and wonder of the created world reflect his creative mind and purpose. We also believe that he must be that Being greater than which there is nothing else. Because we can conceive so strongly of such an idea, and the reality of God must be greater than even this idea, we can be pretty sure that he does exist.

People also claim to experience God in their lives – in prayer, thought, artistic inspiration and unexpected circumstances. We can never know everything about God, of course, but what we can know by thought, experience and love is real and true.

## Doesn't science explain everything today anyway?

Science explains *how* the universe operates in all its variety and splendour. It rests on the assumption that everything is organized in a consistent way that we can understand and investigate by the use of our reason. But science cannot explain *why* the universe exists, or who (or what) created it, or its meaning for human life in the future. Christian belief works in parallel with scientific thought to answer these deeper questions in the light of Jesus and his teaching.

## If God is love, why is there evil and suffering in the world?

This is the most difficult question confronting Christianity, and it has been given added weight by the horrors of recent history. There is no complete answer to this question, which for many people may arise out of traumatic personal experience. However, Christians believe that when God created human beings, he gave them free choice. Like a parent, he cannot force people to be loving and good. Much evil in the world springs from wrong human choices over many centuries – and to some extent, we believe, these have dislocated our relationship with the world of nature too. What happened to Jesus on the Cross reveals that God enters into human suffering to destroy evil, and to offer healing to people through forgiveness and love. Often, in the midst of great evil and suffering, good springs forth in human life in remarkable and courageous ways. Like light in a dark tunnel, this confirms that evil does not always have the last word.

## Doesn't religion cause a lot of conflict in the world?

Religion can cause deep conflict between peoples because at its root the word means 'that which binds a society together'. In situations of tension, religion can be one of the ways in which a society defines and defends itself against a perceived rival or threat. So it may become part of the conflict, along with economic and political issues. Sometimes in history, forms of Christianity have become part of the religious cause of a conflict. But this is actually to twist Christian belief and to distort it for human purposes. Properly understood, Christianity is the antidote to such fatal rivalry between human beings. It teaches us to love other people – even our enemies – and so it holds out the hope of a genuine and lasting reconciliation.

## The Church is irrelevant to modern society

This is often said because modern Western society has given people such a wide choice of activity and the prosperity to pursue individual wishes. The Church, by its nature, is not in a strong position to compete with such a sustained appeal to people's desires. Its message cuts across the hopes of a consumer society, and by its call to self-sacrifice and its compassion for the disadvantaged, it seems to challenge a life of personal success and fulfilment. But certain important social beliefs and values – such as freedom of thought, toleration, social justice, a stable and rational moral order, and charitable concern – rest upon Christianity. These values are not exclusive to Christians, of course. But if the Church were to disappear, they would be seriously undermined. The Church exists to remind people that, in the words of Jesus, 'man is not to live on bread alone, but on every word that comes from the mouth of God' (Matthew 4:4).

## I don't need God anyway!

Of course, what a person believes is their own free and private choice. If we believe that God respects human choice, so should we. We should never try to compel Christian belief. But the above point of view can be gently challenged along these lines:

- Have you spent much time thinking through the question of God?

- What is the purpose of human life?

- Why should a person be good?

- Can human society be rescued from its destructive tendencies?

- If God does not exist, why is there such a strong idea and sense of God in human minds, consciences and cultures?

## It doesn't matter what you believe

One of the harshest questions to arise from recent history is this: How would you persuade a concentration camp guard or terrorist not to murder a child if he or she thought it was the right thing to do? What you believe determines how you behave, for good or ill. It is, of course, possible to construct a moral code of real goodness without a belief in God, but would it have the authority to challenge evil conduct effectively? Christianity believes that loving God goes hand in hand with loving other people, in fulfilment of the Great Commandment (see Mark 12:29–31), and that

95

we are personally accountable to God for how we act. In any human society there must be consensus and discipline based upon law which has a moral basis – otherwise anarchy and corruption set in and society cannot function effectively. So what people believe to be good and true is more than just a private, individual opinion – it affects and determines the basic bond of trust within society.

## What about other religions?

It is important that Christians should stand for toleration and respect for the beliefs and customs of other religions, at home and abroad. This attitude is the hallmark of a free society; it is also a witness to our confidence in Jesus, who called himself 'the Truth'. We believe that God has revealed himself in a full, personal and unique way in Jesus. Jesus affirmed this when he proclaimed himself to be 'the Way, the Truth and the Life', and the only secure road to the knowledge of God as Father (see John 14:6). But he also indicated in his parable about the sheep and the goats (see Matthew 25) that compassion for others marks out those who truly have some sense of God. How people behave, anywhere in the world, expresses most accurately what they believe, for good or ill.

Christianity has a special relationship to Judaism, from which it sprang. Jesus himself was a devout Jew. So too were his earliest disciples, who created the New Testament by interpreting Jesus' life, teaching, death and resurrection against the backdrop that Christians now call the Old Testament. Any attack on the Jews and their beliefs is therefore an indirect attack on Christianity also. Islam has common roots with Judaism and Christianity – all three faiths worship the same God and have many ethical values in common. Jews and Muslims do not, however, accept that Jesus is the Son of God; but this should not lead to antagonism between members of the three faiths.

In most Western countries today there are many Hindus, Sikhs, Buddhists and people of other faiths. It is important that they should feel secure and welcome in our land and in our local communities. The best way to learn about these faiths is to make friends with individuals and to attend their acts of worship. Christians should never be afraid to take a kind and open-hearted interest in this way. When we share our faith in Christ, it must always be in an honest dialogue, where we listen sincerely to what others wish to tell us about what they believe. We in our turn must 'speak the truth in love', and so prove to be true Christians. We must remember that if God respects and invites human freedom of choice in matters of belief, so should we as his ambassadors and servants.

So to be a Christian means believing some important things about human life and its value, and its ultimate purpose in the eyes of God. Being a Christian is an act of thought and trust, relying on the experience of many intelligent and courageous people who have been Christians before us in different, and sometimes difficult, situations. Christianity holds out to human society a real hope of change for the better, built upon freedom, reconciliation and compassion. It enables people to challenge and overcome fear and evil. In many places in the world today, Christians are hard at work putting this vision into practice.

### Prayer

*Eternal light shine into our hearts;*
*eternal goodness deliver us from evil;*
*eternal power be our support;*
*eternal wisdom scatter the darkness of*
*our ignorance;*
*eternal pity have mercy upon us:*
*that with all our heart and mind and soul*
*and strength*
*we may seek thy face*
*and be brought by thine infinite mercy*
*into thy holy presence;*
*through Jesus Christ our Lord.*
*Amen.*

*(Alcuin)*

PART FOUR

# Being with God

# Preparing for Holy Communion

For most people, Confirmation is also the gateway to Holy Communion. This is not always the case in other churches, and in some Anglican churches people are now admitted to Holy Communion before Confirmation. Whatever route we have travelled, when we come to share in Holy Communion we enter into the heart of the Church's life.

The different names for this service in the various branches of the Church highlight different aspects of its meaning:

- 'Eucharist' is from a Greek word which means 'thanksgiving' – giving thanks to God for the gift of Jesus Christ.

- 'Holy Communion' speaks of our holy relationship with God.

- 'Mass' in the Catholic Church probably means 'a common meal', shared with the whole family of God.

- 'Divine Liturgy' in the Orthodox churches means 'worship of God'.

- 'The Lord's Supper' and 'the Breaking of Bread' are Protestant terms springing from the New Testament itself, reminding us of the intimacy of a shared meal.

The important thing to remember is that 'we break this bread to share in the Body of Christ: though we are many, we are one body, because we all share in the one bread'. These words in the Communion service come from St Paul (see 1 Corinthians 10:16–17), and they explain why, as Anglicans, we welcome to Holy Communion all Christians who would normally receive the sacrament in their own church.

Everyone celebrates the Holy Communion together. The priest may be the leading voice, but the celebration rises from the heart of each Christian present. When we celebrate Holy Communion we join with Christians around the world in every church, and those who have lived in history and who are now in heaven: 'with angels and archangels and all the company of heaven, we praise your glorious Name . . .'

It is therefore most important that we prepare

ourselves sincerely and carefully to celebrate and receive Holy Communion – it is one of the most significant things we do each week. How we pray at home will contribute to this; so too will time set aside to consider the readings for the coming Sunday. When we enter a church, we need to remember that the celebration of Holy Communion there makes it the House of God. Whatever else we may have to do before a church service, we should always make time to sit or kneel quietly to prepare ourselves. Remember the picture of the Church as an orchestra; each member has to tune up, but in this case silently!

Here are some prayers that you could say quietly in church before and after Holy Communion (you could even learn them by heart). They are drawn from various traditions within the Church.

## Prayers for use before Communion

*Almighty God,*
*to whom all hearts are open, all desires*
*known,*
*and from whom no secrets are hidden:*
*cleanse the thoughts of our hearts*
*by the inspiration of your Holy Spirit,*
*that we may perfectly love you,*
*and worthily magnify your holy Name.*
*Through Jesus Christ our Lord.*
*Amen.*

*(Book of Common Prayer)*


*Cleanse our consciences, Lord, in your mercy,*
*by the coming of your Holy Spirit:*
*that when your Son, our Lord Jesus Christ,*
*comes to us, he may find in us*
*a holy dwelling-place prepared for himself;*
*for he lives and reigns with you*
*in the unity of the Holy Spirit,*
*one God forever.*
*Amen.*

*(Traditional)*

# Preparing for Holy Communion

*Help us, O Lord our God,*
*to stand before you in purity and holiness,*
*with respect for you,*
*and a sense of the beauty of your Presence:*
*that we may truly and lovingly worship you*
*as Lord and creator of all,*
*Father, Son, and Holy Spirit.*
*Amen.*

*(Orthodox)*


*We have come into your house, O Lord,*
*to serve and worship you*
*in the presence of your whole Church*
*in earth and heaven.*
*O Lamb of God,*
*you offered yourself on the Cross to*
*redeem us all;*
*grant that by your Holy Spirit,*
*we may offer ourselves to you,*
*as a living sacrifice of love, obedience*
*and service.*
*Amen.*

*(Orthodox)*

## This Is My Faith

*Come, Lord, in the dawning,*
*come in the newness of the morning,*
*come, make yourself known at the break of day*
*and in the Breaking of the Bread.    Amen.*

*(Anon)*

## Prayers for use after Communion

*We have celebrated and proclaimed*
*the fullness of your love and salvation*
*for all humanity, O Lord, in this Eucharist:*
*we have held the memorial of your death.*
*We have glimpsed the reality of your*
*resurrection,*
*we have been filled with your unending life,*
*we have sensed the glory*
*of your eternal kingdom and its joy.*
*Make us worthy by your Holy Spirit*
*of your perfect love,*
*direct our paths aright,*
*and root us firmly in reverence for you.*
*Grant that we may come in the end*
*to your eternal kingdom in heaven,*
*through Jesus Christ, your Son, our Lord.*
*Amen.*

*(Orthodox)*

## Preparing for Holy Communion

*O Lord Jesus Christ,*
*in this wonderful sacrament,*
*you have left us a memorial*
*of your cross and resurrection:*
*help us so to receive the sacred mysteries*
*of your Body and Blood,*
*that we may sense in our hearts,*
*and show forth in our lives*
*the fruits of your Holy Spirit.*
*Amen.*

*(Traditional)*


*Lord Jesus Christ,*
*I need only one thing in this world:*
*to know myself and to love you.*
*Give me day by day your grace and your love;*
*for with these I am rich enough,*
*I desire nothing more.*
*Amen.*

*(Pope John XXIII)*

# The Shape of the Eucharist

Everything in the Eucharist or Holy Communion service has a meaning and also a history. Two pictures can help us to think about this – a great piece of music and an old cathedral. The more we understand the music and its background, the better we shall be able to play it or appreciate it. The more we let it soak into our lives, the more truly and deeply we shall be able to express it to others. Again, if we enter a very old cathedral, every nook and cranny has its own atmosphere and meaning. Such buildings can give us a keen sense of Christian history in a way that guides and inspires us today.

## The roots

The roots of the Eucharist take us back to the very beginnings of Christianity in the Jewish synagogues of the first century after Christ. Each week, Jews met to worship God and to celebrate his faithfulness to their people over long centuries of history, as they still do today. Once a year, around Easter time, they celebrate the Passover, to commemorate the Exodus from Egypt, which was the defining moment of the Jewish people and their faith. In early Christianity, these two elements were gradually woven together, as Christian Jews met to celebrate the death and resurrection of Jesus. Each Sunday, the first day of the new week, is an echo of Easter itself, and a reminder of the coming new age of God's eternal kingdom.

The earliest written record of this process is in St Paul's first letter to the church at Corinth in Greece (1 Corinthians chapters 10 and 11). The origins of this weekly commemoration of Jesus can be found in the accounts of the Last Supper in the Gospels (e.g. Mark 14:12–25). So today, the first part of the Eucharist recalls the Jewish synagogue's service of worship, prayers and Bible readings. The second part re-enacts the Last Supper, calling to mind the death and resurrection of Jesus.

There is now great similarity between the Anglican, Catholic, Lutheran and Methodist services of Holy Communion – all are modelled on a renewed understanding of the early forms of the Eucharist. This is an important sign of the underlying unity of the Church, and it means that wherever we go in the world, we can easily feel at home in such a service, even if it is in a foreign language. The Orthodox liturgy is longer and more elaborate, but very moving. It conveys strongly the holiness of God.

At the end of this book, (page 135) you will find one of the modern Anglican services of Holy Communion, taken from *Common Worship*. It is modelled on the oldest known liturgy, the rite of St Hippolytus, which comes from Rome around the year 200 AD. This underlies the pattern of Anglican and Roman celebrations today.

## The ministry of the Word

To travel through the service of Holy Communion is to sense the history and the rich spiritual experience of the Christian Church. In the Anglican service, the opening 'Collect for purity' has been in use in England for over a thousand years. The 'Kyries' ('Lord have mercy') were introduced into the service in the early fourth century, when it was in Greek. The 'Gloria' is an ancient morning hymn of the Church; originally it was in Greek, then it was in Latin, and finally it was translated into English at the time of the Reformation. Many of the 'Collects' or prayers for the day are translations of ancient Latin prayers that were written in Rome before Christianity came to England, though some of them are more modern.

The readings from the Bible are often linked together by some seasonal theme – for example, Christmas or Easter, or a saint's day. There may be a psalm between the readings from the Old and New Testaments. Then a canticle from the New Testament, or a hymn, may precede the Gospel itself. These readings remind us of God's continual dialogue with his people, Israel and the Church. The sermon should draw together the meaning of these readings and should apply them to Christian life today.

On Sundays and major festivals, everyone recites the Nicene Creed, the statement of what Christians everywhere believe. This has been done in the Church for over a thousand years, and it reminds us of the rich and universal tradition of faith to which we are heirs. Then come the Intercessions, which are prayers for the Church, the world, the community, those in need, and those who have died. The 'litany form' of these prayers by which we all respond is a very old form of congregational participation.

Holy Communion is never received without a formal, public act of confession of sins. This may occur at the start of the service, or after the prayers. It reminds us that we cannot enter God's presence or receive his gifts to us unless we are truly sorry for what we have done wrong, and are willing to change. This moment in church pulls us up short, and sharply reminds us that, in the words of St Paul, 'all alike have sinned and are deprived of the divine glory' (Romans 3:23). It is in this spirit of repentance that we offer to each other the sign of Peace, expressing our commitment to reconciliation and forgiveness, and making each other truly welcome in church.

## The ministry of the Sacrament

The second part of the service starts with the offering of bread and wine, and often of money too. This reminds us that all of life is God's gift to us. How do we respond to his generosity towards us – not just at this moment, but each day, and in all our attitudes and values?

The great prayer of thanksgiving begins with praise to God for creating the world, and for sending Jesus to save us and to show us God's love. It also commemorates the giving of the Holy Spirit, and sometimes includes a reference to the particular season or feast that is being celebrated. We affirm this act of worship and thanksgiving in the words of the 'Sanctus' and the 'Benedictus': 'Holy, Holy, Holy, Lord God of hosts: heaven and earth are full of your glory . . . Blessed is he who comes in the Name of the Lord.' These words are drawn from the Bible – from the prophet Isaiah's vision of God in the Temple (Isaiah 6:3), and from the psalms that were used to acclaim Jesus as he entered Jerusalem on Palm Sunday (Psalm 118:26; see Luke 19:38). In these words we worship God – Father, Son and Holy Spirit – with reverence and love.

The prayer then moves on to recall with great simplicity and solemnity the Last Supper, and the actual words that Jesus said over the bread and the wine: 'This is my Body . . . this is my Blood.' We pray for the coming of the Holy Spirit to make this real for us. The prayer ends by calling to mind all that Jesus accomplished in history, and the hope that he holds out to his Church for the present and for the future.

The great consecrating prayer of thanksgiving is then followed by the Lord's Prayer. It was placed there by St Gregory the Great in the sixth century. It is the prayer that unites all Christians everywhere with Christ and with each other. This is followed by the Breaking of Bread: this recalls again the death of Jesus, which restores peace and unity to human beings, beginning in the Church. This is celebrated in the words of the 'Agnus Dei': 'Lamb of God, you take away the sins of the world: have mercy on us' (see John 1:29). This ancient hymn has been in use since the seventh century in the Western Church.

Then comes the moment of Communion itself. This may be received either kneeling or standing, and in the Anglican Church people usually receive both the bread and the wine. In the moment of Communion, God offers himself to us in Jesus by the power of the Holy Spirit, as we open our hearts and offer ourselves to him. This is the most personal part of the whole service.

The Eucharist ends with some final prayers of thanksgiving and commitment, and perhaps a hymn, and then the Blessing. We are sent out into the world, where we live and work, to take the presence of Christ with us, to shine as lights in the world to the glory of God – Father, Son and Holy Spirit.

# In His Presence

The Eucharist is like a profound piece of music, compiled and enriched over many centuries of use. Because it speaks about God and his love for human beings expressed in the person of Jesus, it is not really possible to sum up its meaning altogether. It uses the language of worship, poetry and love, and to enter into it is to draw close to the mystery of God himself, as Father, Son and Holy Spirit. Its meaning will unfold to us, like the meaning of the Bible also, over many years of prayer and experience. We shall find that the Eucharist stands at the very heart of being a Christian in the Church.

To celebrate the Eucharist is to stand on the threshold between time and eternity. We worship God with the whole company of worshippers on earth and in heaven, as with them we proclaim, 'Holy, Holy, Holy.' The royal and solemn nature of this great act of worship reminds us that we stand in the presence of God, the Creator and

Ruler of all that exists. We may well come to sense this in unforgettable ways, which will begin to alter our whole perspective on life and its meaning.

The Eucharist is a corporate act – no individual can celebrate it alone. It builds up the life of the local church and links it to the wider Church throughout the world and throughout history. It can be celebrated anywhere – in a church or a cathedral, in a home or a hospital, in the open air or even on a battlefield. It can truly be celebrated 'at all times and in all places', bringing our life into communion with God and his people everywhere. It is also a drama, in which actions interpret words. We need both to listen and to watch, as the whole meaning of the gospel is set before us in a healing and uplifting way, which may touch and transform our own lives and the lives of others.

But the Eucharist is also an intensely private and personal act of devotion and love to Christ. Week by week, it renews the commitment that we made at Baptism and Confirmation. It is the sacrament that deepens our own personal relationship with Jesus Christ. To him we bring our hopes and fears, our joys and sorrows, and our own private prayers and thoughts. That is why we should never come to Holy Communion unprepared.

*Lord, I am not worthy to receive you;*
*But only speak the word, and I shall be healed.*

The word 'Eucharist' means 'thanksgiving', and gratitude should lie at the heart of our relationship – our 'holy communion' – with God. The great consecrating prayer of thanksgiving is central to the whole service. We stand in the presence of God to recognize all that he has done for us, and to thank him in a loving and sincere way. This spirit of gratitude inspires the generosity which is the hallmark of being truly Christian. We are called to relate to God freely for who he is, not just for what he may do for us. Herein lies the key to any true relationship between persons. We must never take God for granted, nor the life and love that he has given us in Jesus Christ.

At the heart of the consecrating prayer is the solemn commemoration of the sacrifice made by Jesus on the Cross for the salvation of human beings. The words of the Last Supper point to this awesome event. We recognize that he died for us – words that are echoed when we are called to come forward to receive Communion. In a deep and mysterious way, the moment of the consecration of the bread and the wine draws us very close to the events of that Last Supper, and to God's eternal sacrifice revealed in Jesus upon the Cross of Calvary. Our life is at that moment joined to Christ's own self-sacrifice and love, and his blessings flow into our lives to enable us to be self-sacrificing also.

*Behold, I am the servant of the Lord:*
*May it be unto me according to your word.*

All Christians believe and sense that in some wonderful way, Christ makes himself present by his Spirit during Holy Communion. They may express it in different ways, but this is why the Eucharist has always been treasured at the heart of the Church's life. We come together to meet him, and to receive afresh his Spirit in our lives. For it is the Holy Spirit who makes Christ real, through the pages of the Gospels, and in the sacrament of Communion. That is why receiving Communion should be protected by silence and time for reflection. This sacrament is the miracle sustaining the life of the Church, because it communicates to us the risen life of Christ himself. It provides food and refreshment for us on our life-long journey towards God's eternal kingdom in heaven.

The word 'Communion' indicates a relationship – a holy relationship with God and with others. As we respond to God's great love for us, we offer ourselves in a simple and sincere way to become the dwelling-place of his Spirit. In this self-offering we also pray for those with whom we have any kind of relationship – all whom we love and serve. They are present with us at this moment of Communion, even if not in an immediate, physical way. We take Christ to them by our prayers and attitudes, our words and actions, all of which should be inspired by our receiving of Holy Communion. At the end of the service we are encouraged to go forth in peace to love and serve Christ in others in his name.

**Prayer**

*Almighty God, we thank you for feeding
us
with the Body and Blood of your Son,
Jesus Christ our Lord:
through him we offer you our souls and
bodies
to be a living sacrifice.
Send us out in the power of your Holy
Spirit
To live and work to your praise and glory.
Amen.*

*(Common Worship)*

# Ambassadors for Christ

St Paul defined Christians as 'ambassadors for Christ . . . as if God were making his appeal through you' (2 Corinthians 5:20). These are amazing words. How can we truly be ambassadors for Christ? What a responsibility! Yet we go forth from Holy Communion with Christ in the heart of our lives, called to be people in whom his Holy Spirit dwells, and through whom his life and love may be sensed by others.

As we reflect on all that we have learned in preparation for Confirmation and Holy Communion, four central symbols stand out. They hold before us a vision of what it means to be a Christian.

## The water of life

Baptism is about being dipped in water in the name of God, Father, Son and Holy Spirit. The promises that we make then and renew at

Confirmation should guide us every day as Christians. Do I turn to Christ? Do I repent of my sins? Do I reject evil? Christianity is built on the foundation laid at Baptism, and the water signifies the three parts of this foundation.

The first is forgiveness. This is where we start. We have to face up to our sins and accept God's love and forgiveness of us, like the Prodigal Son (see Luke chapter 15). By the water of Baptism, the Holy Spirit removes the dead weight of our sin and guilt.

The second is cleansing. Just as it is vital to drink clean water, so it is vital that we become free from sin and open to God's purifying love. He wishes to restore to us the holiness of life for which we were originally created, and without which we shall never be truly happy.

The third is eternal life. This is the great hope and promise of the gospel. The goal of our existence is not restricted to this earthly life. Instead this life, in the loving hands of God, becomes a preparation for eternal life in his kingdom of heaven.

Whoever drinks the water that I shall give will never again be thirsty. The water that I shall

give will be a spring of water within him,
welling up and bringing eternal life.

*(John 4:14)*

## The cup of salvation

When you see the chalice placed on the altar, prepared to receive the water and wine for Holy
Communion, you see a symbol of yourself. You
too are carefully made of precious material for a
holy purpose. Like a chalice in church, you have
to be clean, stable and completely open to
heaven, in order that God's Spirit may fill your
heart and life with the living fire of his love.

The chalice often has a large knob in the
middle, to help people hold it securely when they
give the wine to communicants. We have to be
prepared to allow God to have a firm but loving
grip on our lives, so that through us he can give
his love to other people. The chalice reminds us
that what we receive from God we are called to
give to others in service, prayer and compassion.

In the Gospels, the chalice is also a symbol of
following Christ along the way of the Cross. It
reminds us that to be a Christian will involve
suffering in various ways from time to time. Jesus

made this quite clear to his disciples, and at Baptism and Confirmation we are hallmarked with the sign of the Cross.

> Can you drink the cup that I drink, or be baptised with the baptism I am baptised with?
>
> *(Mark 10:38)*

## The bread of heaven

Bread is the staple food in most human societies. It is produced by many different people from a natural crop, and it is something that we share with others when we sit down to a meal, or when we see someone in need. For Christians, bread takes on a special meaning in the light of its consecration in Holy Communion. It becomes a picture of the whole shape of Christian life.

Jesus spoke about harvest as the time when God would weigh up the quality of our lives, as in the Parable of the Sower (see Mark 4:1–20). We are called to bring forth the fruits of God's Spirit. But to make bread you have first to crush the seed. Even when we think we have achieved something in the Christian life, God may act decisively, apparently turning everything upside down!

Water, oil, salt and yeast must be added to the flour. In the Gospels, these are all images of God's kingdom and of the hidden work of his Holy Spirit. They transform the whole mixture, as God's own eternal life is joined to our life in an irreversible union of love. Then the dough is kneaded – a stretching process that transforms its whole structure again. Being in the hands of the living God is not always a comfortable experience!

Finally, the dough is left in a dark place to rise, before being baked in an oven in order to become a life-giving substance. This is a powerful picture of what Christians believe about death as the gateway to eternal life. There is a real dying, but it is in the end life-giving, as was true in the death and resurrection of Jesus himself.

I am the bread of life. Whoever comes to me will never be hungry, and whoever believes in me will never be thirsty. *(John 6:35)*

## The fruits of the Spirit

St Paul taught that the hallmarks of Christian life are the 'fruit of God's Spirit' (Galatians 5:22–23), which in the end make us like Christ himself – love, joy, peace, patience, kindness, goodness, gentleness and self-control. These qualities require great inner strength, and at times real faith as well. It is no easy thing to love others as we would wish to be loved ourselves. Jesus defined this further as loving them as he has loved us – even to the point of loving and forgiving our enemies and those who have hurt us, as he did on the Cross.

This means that how we live our lives as Christians is of supreme importance. God values us highly; but he also values others equally highly. Our attitudes have to be corrected in the light of Jesus, so that our words and actions are consistent expressions of God's compassion. If we deliberately hurt others or betray them, we may make it harder for them to accept God's love and forgiveness. We are indeed called to be responsible for our brothers and sisters, valuing them as God's children. We cannot simply pass them by.

This sense of vocation and duty should guide

us in how we form our relationships. Friends and family matter greatly, of course; but so too does the stranger and the foreigner. Falling in love is wonderful; but casual sexual activity may well reduce our chances of having a happy marriage and of being able to provide a secure family life for our children yet to be. This, in the end, would be a denial of love. Valuing other people, and respecting their right to space, privacy and independence is an important key to relationships; so too is forgiveness. Being there for people in a reliable and compassionate way is another key. All this requires great unselfishness, but it mirrors the constancy of God himself.

This sense of vocation should also guide how we form our careers and spend our money. Every Christian has a duty to contribute positively to the life of society, and also to the life of the Church, by their prayers and by giving generously of their time, money and skills. We do not live just for ourselves, and so we need to organize our lives so that this life of service to others is possible.

Some Christians may feel called by God quite specifically to serve him and humanity in the work of medicine, education or social care, either at home or abroad. Some may feel him calling them to become priests, monks or nuns. These are all careers that any Christian should from time to time seriously consider. Does God want me to offer my life to him in this way?

But whatever occupation we pursue, we are each called, with the help of the Holy Spirit, to live the Christian life to the full, and to see all that we do as an act of service in fulfilment of God's loving call to us. He has a plan for our lives which, if we sincerely seek and accept it, will always be in our true interests. We shall then discover that, whatever happens, nothing will be able to separate us from God's love for us in Jesus Christ.

*O God, the protector of all who trust in you, without whom nothing is strong, nothing is holy; pour upon us your mercy and be our ruler and guide, that we may so pass through life in this world that we attain the life of your eternal kingdom. Grant this, O Heavenly Father, for the sake of Jesus Christ, your Son, our Lord. Amen.*

(Book of Common Prayer)

## Ambassadors for Christ

Lord, make me an instrument of your peace.
Where there is hatred, let me sow love;
where there is injury, pardon;
where there is doubt, faith;
where there is despair, hope;
where there is darkness, light;
where there is sadness, joy.

O Divine Master, grant that I may not so
much seek
to be consoled as to console,
to be understood as to understand,
to be loved as to love.

For it is in giving that we receive,
it is in pardoning that we are pardoned,
and it is in dying daily to Christ that we are
born to eternal life.

*(Prayer of St Francis)*

# An Order of Holy Communion

The order of service which follows is Holy Communion Order One (incorporating Eucharistic Prayer B) from *Common Worship: Services and Prayers for the Church of England*.

It is introduced here by Bishop David Stancliffe, Chairman of the Liturgical Commission of the Church of England and Bishop of Salisbury.

The pattern for Order One has four main sections:

**The Gathering,** during which the assembly is constituted by singing or saying together the opening prayers, is recalled in penitence to its baptismal status, and is prepared to receive the Word of God. This section is summed up in the Collect.

**The Liturgy of the Word,** during which the assembly engages with the Word, as the story of what God has done in Christ is set alongside the community's experience, and in the Sermon its implications are drawn out for prayer and action.

**The Liturgy of the Sacrament,** during which the assembly is offered the possibility of transformation as it is incorporated into the one, perfect self-offering of Christ to the Father, and receives the body and blood of Christ in faith with thanksgiving.

**The Dismissal,** when the assembly is reminded to put into practice the new life it has received, and is sent out into the community to do so.

† David Sarum

# Holy Communion

*Responses are in bold type*

## The Greeting

Lord be with you
**And also with you.**

## Prayer of Preparation

Almighty God,
to whom all hearts are open,
all desires known,
and from whom no secrets are hidden:
cleanse the thoughts of our hearts
by the inspiration of your Holy Spirit,
that we may perfectly love you,
and worthily magnify your holy name;
through Christ our Lord.
Amen.

## Prayers of Penitence

*(After a seasonal or other form of invitation to confession)*

Let us confess our sins in penitence and faith,
Firmly resolved to keep God's commandments
And to live in love and peace with all.

Almighty God, our heavenly Father,
we have sinned against you
and against our neighbour
in thought and word and deed,
through negligence, through weakness,
through our own deliberate fault.
We are truly sorry
and repent of all our sins.
For the sake of your Son Jesus Christ,
who died for us,
forgive us all that is past
and grant that we may serve you in newness of
    life
to the glory of your name.
Amen.

Almighty God.
who forgives all who truly repent,
have mercy upon you,
pardon and deliver you from all your sins,
confirm and strengthen you in all goodness,
and keep you in life eternal;
through Jesus Christ our Lord
**Amen.**

## The Kyries

Lord, have mercy.
**Lord, have mercy.**

Christ, have mercy.
**Christ, have mercy.**

Lord, have mercy.
**Lord, have mercy.**

## Gloria in Excelsis

**Glory to God in the highest,**
**and peace to his people on earth.**

**Lord God, heavenly King,**
**almighty God and Father,**
**we worship you, we give you thanks,**
**we praise you for your glory.**

Lord Jesus Christ, only Son of the Father,
Lord God, Lamb of God,
you take away the sin of the world:
have mercy on us;
you are seated at the right hand of the Father:
receive our prayer.

For you alone are the Holy One,
you alone are the Lord,
you alone are the Most High, Jesus Christ,
with the Holy Spirit,
in the glory of God the Father.
Amen.

## The Collect

*(The prayer for the day which alters according
to the seasons)*

Amen.

## The Readings

*(One or two readings from the Bible, sometimes
with a psalm or hymn between)*

## Gospel Reading

*(Following the ancient custom of the Church, we stand for the Gospel)*

## The Sermon

## The Nicene Creed

We believe in one God,
the Father, the Almighty, Maker of heaven and
   earth,
of all that is,
seen and unseen.

We believe in one Lord, Jesus Christ,
the only son of God,
eternally begotten of the Father,
God from God, Light from Light,
true God from true God,
begotten, not made,
of one being with the Father;
through him all things were made.
For us and for our salvation he came down from
   heaven,

was incarnate from the Holy Spirit and the
  Virgin Mary
and was made man.
For our sake he was crucified under Pontius
  Pilate;
he suffered death and was buried.
On the third day he rose again
in accordance with the Scriptures;
he ascended into heaven
and is seated at the right hand of the Father.
He will come again in glory to judge the living
  and the dead,
and his kingdom will have no end.

We believe in the Holy Spirit,
the Lord, the giver of life,
who proceeds from the Father and the Son,
who with the Father and the Son is worshipped
  and glorified,
who has spoken through the prophets.
We believe in one holy catholic and apostolic
  Church.
We acknowledge one baptism for the forgiveness
  of sins.
We look for the resurrection of the dead,
and the life of the world to come. Amen.

## Prayers of Intercession

## The Peace

*(This may be introduced by a seasonal sentence)*

The peace of the Lord be always with you
**And also with you.**

## Preparation of the Table – taking of the Bread and the Wine

*(Prayers may be said over the gifts of bread and wine)*

## The Eucharistic Prayer

The Lord be with you
**And also with you.**

Lift up your hearts.
**We lift them to the Lord.**

Let us give thanks to the Lord our God.
**It is right to give thanks and praise.**

Father, we give you thanks and praise
through your beloved Son Jesus Christ, your
    living Word,
through whom you have created all things;
who was sent by you in your great goodness to
    be our Saviour.

By the power of the Holy Spirit he took flesh;
as your Son, born of the blessed Virgin,
he lived on earth and went about among us;
he opened wide his arms for us on the cross;
he put an end to death by dying for us;
and revealed the resurrection by rising to new
    life;
so he fulfilled your will and won for you a holy
    people.

*(A short seasonal preface may be included here)*

Therefore with angels and archangels,
and with all the company of heaven,
we proclaim your great and glorious name.
for ever praising you and saying:

**Holy, holy, holy Lord,**
**God of power and might,**
**heaven and earth are full of your glory.**
**Hosanna in the highest.**

**Blessed is he who comes in the name of the Lord.**
**Hosanna in the highest.**

Lord, you are holy indeed, the source of all
holiness;
grant that by the power of your Holy Spirit,
and according to your holy will,
these gifts of bread and wine
may be to us the body and blood of our Lord
Jesus Christ;
who, in the same night that he was betrayed,
took bread and gave you thanks;
he broke it and gave it to his disciples, saying:
Take eat; this is my body which is given for you;
do this in remembrance of me.

In the same way, after supper
he took the cup and gave you thanks;
he gave it to them, saying:
Drink this, all of you;
this is my blood of the new covenant,
which is shed for you and for many for the
forgiveness of sins.
Do this, as often as you drink it,
in remembrance of me.

## This Is My Faith

Great is the mystery of faith:
**Christ has died:**
**Christ is risen:**
**Christ will come again.**

And so, Father, calling to mind his death on the
  cross,
his perfect sacrifice made once for the sins of the
  whole world;
rejoicing in his mighty resurrection and glorious
  ascension,
and looking for his coming in glory,
we celebrate this memorial of our redemption.
As we offer you this our sacrifice of praise and
  thanksgiving,
we bring before you this bread and this cup
and we thank you for counting us worthy
to stand in your presence and serve you.

Send the Holy Spirit on your people
and gather into one in your kingdom
all who share in this one bread and one cup,
so that we, in the company of all the saints,
may praise and glorify you for ever,
through Jesus Christ our Lord;

by whom, and with whom, and in whom,
in the unity of the Holy Spirit,
all honour and glory be yours, almighty Father,
for ever and ever.
**Amen.**

## The Lord's Prayer

As our Saviour taught us, so we pray

**Our Father, who art in heaven,
hallowed be thy name;
thy kingdom come;
thy will be done;
on earth as it is in heaven.
Give us this day our daily bread.
And forgive us our trespasses,
as we forgive those who trespass against us.
And lead us not into temptation;
but deliver us from evil.
For thine is the kingdom,
the power and the glory,
for ever and ever.
Amen.**

## Breaking of the Bread

We break this bread
to share in the body of Christ.

Though we are many, we are one body,
because we all share in the one bread.

Lamb of God,
you take away the sin of the world,
have mercy upon us.

Lamb of God,
you take away the sin of the world,
have mercy on us.

Lamb of God,
you take away the sin of the world,
grant us your peace.

## Giving of Communion

Draw near with faith.
Receive the body of our Lord Jesus Christ
which he gave for you,
and his blood which he shed for you.

Eat and drink
in remembrance that he died for you.
and feed on him in your hearts
by faith with thanksgiving.

*(Those who wish to now go forward to receive
Holy Communion)*

## Prayer after Communion

*(A seasonal prayer is said first; then one of these
prayers follows)*

Almighty God,
we thank you for feeding us
with the body and blood of your Son Jesus Christ.
Through him we offer you our souls and bodies
to be a living sacrifice.
Send us out in the power of your Spirit
to live and work
to your praise and glory.
Amen.

Father of all,
we give you thanks and praise,
what when we were still far off
you met us in your Son and brought us home.

Dying and living, he declared your love,
gave us grace, and opened the gate of glory.
May we who share Christ's body live his risen life;
we who drink his cup give life to others;
we whom the Spirit lights give light to the world.
Keep us firm in the hope you have set before us,
so we and all your children shall be free,
and the whole earth live to praise your name;
through Christ our Lord.
Amen.

## Blessing and Dismissal

*(A seasonal blessing may be used, or else this form)*

The peace of God,
which passes all understanding,
keep your hearts and minds
in the knowledge and love of God,
and of his Son Jesus Christ our Lord;
and the blessing of God almighty,
the Father, the Son, and the Holy Spirit,
be among you and remain with you always.
**Amen.**

Go in peace to love and serve the Lord.
**In the name of Christ. Amen.**

# A Little Dictionary of
# the Church

## The Church Building

| | |
|---|---|
| *Altar* | Table for Holy Communion |
| *Aumbrey* | Small cupboard in wall of church used for holy vessels |
| *Chancel* | Area leading to altar where choir sit |
| *Font* | Place of Baptism (from Latin word for 'spring of water') |
| *Nave* | Seating for congregation (from Latin word for 'upturned ship') |
| *Pulpit* | Raised place for preaching |
| *Sanctuary* | Area around altar, railed off |
| *Stained Glass* | Used in windows to depict stories from Bible and saint's lives |
| *Tabernacle* | Locked cupboard where reserved Holy Communion is kept |
| *Transept* | Area either side of junction between chancel and nave |

## Holy Communion

| | |
|---|---|
| *Chalice* | Silver cup used only for Holy Communion |
| *Chrism* | Special oil used by bishop at Confirmation |
| *Corporal* | Linen cloth spread under chalice and patten |
| *Incense* | Scented gum burnt during time of prayer. An ancient tradition found in the Old Testament, symbolizing the prayer of God's people rising to heaven |
| *Intinction* | Receiving the bread dipped into the wine, often used by sick communicants |
| *Missal* | Book on altar containing the order of Holy Communion |
| *Pall* | Linen cover for chalice |
| *Patten* | Silver plate used only for Holy Communion |
| *Purificator* | Linen cloth for wiping chalice during Holy Communion |
| *Pyx* | Small silver box for carrying the bread of Holy Communion to the sick |

## Orders of Ministry

| | |
|---|---|
| *Bishop* | The chief minister looking after a diocese |

# A Little Dictionary of the Church

| | |
|---|---|
| *Priest* | A person ordained to lead a church and celebrate Holy Communion |
| *Deacon* | A person ordained to preach and to serve others in the name of the Church |
| *Lay-Reader* | A person trained and permitted to preach and lead certain services |
| *Monk* | A man dedicated to living the monastic life |
| *Nun* | A woman dedicated to living the monastic life |
| *Church Army Officer* | A person trained for special pastoral ministry with the Church Army |
| *Evangelist* | A person trained to communicate the Gospel |
| *Choir-master* | A person in charge of music and the choir; sometimes also the organist |
| *Church Warden* | A senior lay-person elected annually to help lead and care for the church |

## Vestments

| | |
|---|---|
| *Alb* | Long white robe, symbolizing purity, worn for the celebration of Holy Communion |
| *Cassock* | Long black robe worn by clergy and choir. A bishop's cassock is purple |
| *Chasuble* | Coloured over-garment worn at the celebration of Holy Communion, said |

|          | to represent the seamless garment worn by Christ |
| -------- | ------------------------------------------------ |
| *Cope*     | Long, coloured cloak worn by priests at festivals and ceremonies |
| *Frontal*  | Coloured material hung over the front of the altar to signify the seasons of the Christian year (see below) |
| *Hood*     | Symbol of university degree worn by priests and lay-readers |
| *Mitre*    | Special hat of a bishop, shaped like a flame and symbolizing the Holy Spirit |
| *Stole*    | Coloured band of material worn by deacons, priests and bishops, their 'badge of office'. It is often embroidered and coloured to correspond to the liturgical season (see below) |
| *Surplice* | Long white robe worn over a cassock |
| *Tippet*   | Black scarf worn by priests and lay-readers |

## Seasonal Colours

| | |
| ------- | ------------------------------------------------ |
| *White*  | for feasts of our Lord (e.g. Christmas, Easter) and principal holy days |
| *Red*    | for feasts of the Holy Spirit, Palm Sunday, and feasts of apostles and martyrs |
| *Purple* | for Advent and Lent |
| *Green*  | for Ordinary time through the year |